INTRODUCTION

Welcome to your *New Geography in Action* Portfolio!

You can use this Portfolio to:

- Help you prepare for your classroom-based assessments
- Create and store fantastic examples of your work
- Reflect on your learning and your use of the Junior Cycle Key Skills
- Complete self-assessment checklists
- Develop action plans based on your self-assessment.

We hope you enjoy using your Portfolio!

GW00760517

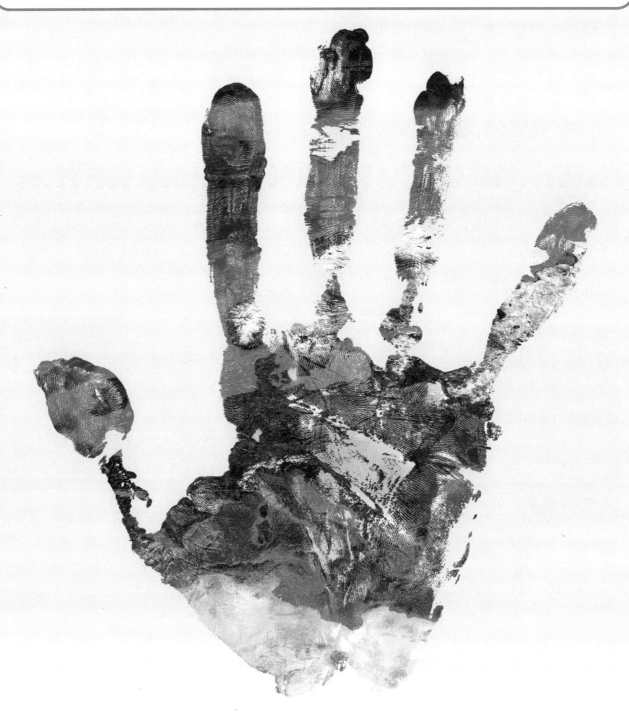

Geographical Skills for First Years: Ordnance Survey and graph skills

SELF-ASSESSMENT

		Page	🙂	😐	☹️
1	I understand how to read OS maps and the scale and national grid they use.	13			
2	I am able to locate a position on an OS map using four-figure grid references and six-figure grid references.	13			
3	I can use the OS legend to identify features on OS maps.	13			
4	I am able to identify height and give directions on an OS map.	13			
5	I can draw a sketch of an OS map.	13			
6	I can read and interpret data from bar charts, pie charts and trend graphs.	17			
7	I can draw bar charts, pie charts and trend graphs.	17			

Write down examples of when you used the following Key Skills in this chapter:	
Being Literate	
Being Numerate	
Being Creative	
Managing Information and Thinking	
Working with Others	
Communicating	
Managing Myself	
Staying Well	

New Geography in Action

Junior Cycle Geography

Portfolio

Norma Lenihan & Jason O'Brien

educate.ie

PUBLISHED BY:

Educate.ie
Walsh Educational Books Ltd
Castleisland, Co. Kerry, Ireland
www.educate.ie

PRINTED AND BOUND BY:
Walsh Colour Print,
Castleisland, Co. Kerry, Ireland

ISBN: 978-1-912239-42-9

ACKNOWLEDGEMENTS

For permission to reproduce artwork, the authors and publisher
acknowledge the following copyright holders:
© ALAMY LTD: Gavin Dronfield / Alamy Stock Photo 44, 45;
Hans Blossey / Alamy Stock Photo 48, 49 ·
© ISTOCKPHOTO.COM: oaltindag / iStockphoto.com 88, 89 ·
© SHUTTERSTOCK INC: Shebeko / Shutterstock 1; Jason Winter /
Shutterstock 6, 7; Ocskay Bence / Shutterstock 10,
11; Creative Idea / Shutterstock 12, 13 (background);
Artography / Shutterstock 13; vadik4444 / Shutterstock 16, 17;
Mimadeo / Shutterstock 02, 21; shutterupeire / Shutterstock
24, 25; Lysogor Roman / Shutterstock 26, 27; Pavel L Photo
and Video / Shutterstock 32, 33; Smiltena / Shutterstock 36,
37; katykin / Shutterstock 52, 53; lavizzara / Shutterstock 54,
55; volcano / Shutterstock 58, 59; ChrisVanLennepPhoto /
Shutterstock 64, 65; Gabriela Insuratelu / Shutterstock 68, 69;
Kubko / Shutterstock 72, 73; Nicolas Economou / Shutterstock
76, 77; StepanPopov / Shutterstock 78, 79; Kaikoro /
Shutterstock 82, 83; Rvector / Shutterstock 84, 85.

Contents

Portfolio

SECTION 3: THIRD YEAR

REFLECTION

List the Topics you know well here:

List the Topics you do not fully understand here:

List the Topics you have difficulty with here:

Write down your Revision Action Plan for this chapter here:

2 The Earth's Surface: Shaping the crust

PORTFOLIO ACTIVITY 2.1: VOLCANO TOURISM LEAFLET

Volcanoes can have positive and negative effects on a region, as you have seen.
Prepare a tourism leaflet for a volcanic region in the space provided. Follow the instructions below:

- Make sure to name your volcano and the country and region it is located in.
- State why the volcano occurs there.
- Outline the positives and negatives for the region.
- Include any photographs, newspaper cuttings, facts and figures to support your promotion of the volcano and its surrounding region.

 For this task you must research a volcano that is currently **active**!

Volcano name and location

_____

KEY SKILLS

I used these two key skills during this portfolio activity:

_____   _____

PORTFOLIO ACTIVITY 2.2: EARTHQUAKE NEWSPAPER REPORT

Write a newspaper report on an earthquake in a developing or developed country. Follow the instructions below:

- Look for images of earthquakes in developed or developing countries.
- Name and locate your example.
- Make a note of the strength of the earthquake.
- List facts and statistics about the damage caused (e.g. death toll, collapsed buildings, infrastructure damage, cost to government).
- List any long-term effects.
- Describe the short-term and long-term responses to the earthquake.

Headline _____

Reporter's name _____

Go through your newspaper reports in groups and create a comparison chart to show the advantages of living in a developed country rather than a developing country when an earthquake strikes.

KEY SKILLS

I used these two key skills during this portfolio activity:

_____   _____

SELF-ASSESSMENT

		Page	🙂	😐	☹️
1	I can name and describe the layers of the Earth.	21			
2	I can explain what plates are and how they move.	23			
3	I can give evidence to prove the theory of plate tectonics.	23			
4	I can explain what happens at each type of plate boundary	23			
5	I can name and describe three features of volcanic activity.	28			
6	I can list the three different types of volcano.	28			
7	I can explain the socio-economic impacts of volcanoes for a region that I have studied.	28			
8	I can describe the impact of a volcano and how people respond to this natural disaster.	28			
9	I can explain how earthquakes occur and how they are measured.	31			
10	I can describe the impact of an earthquake and how people respond to this natural disaster.	31			
11	I can explain how fold mountains are formed.	34			
12	I can say when fold mountains were formed.	34			
13	I can describe how people make a living in mountainous areas.	34			

Write down examples of when you used the following Key Skills in this chapter:	
Being Literate	
Being Numerate	
Being Creative	
Managing Information and Thinking	
Working with Others	
Communicating	
Managing Myself	
Staying Well	

REFLECTION

List the Topics you know well here:

List the Topics you do not fully understand here:

List the Topics you have difficulty with here:

Write down your Revision Action Plan for this chapter here:

3 Rocks: How they are formed and used

PORTFOLIO ACTIVITY 3.1: ROCKS, THE LANDSCAPE AND TOURISM

Go to **www.giantscausewayofficialguide.com** *to find out why the Giant's Causeway is one of the most important tourist attractions in Northern Ireland. Write an article for a tourist magazine encouraging people to visit.*

Rocks: How they are formed and used

 KEY SKILLS

I used these two key skills during this portfolio activity:

_____   _____

PORTFOLIO ACTIVITY 3.2: ROCK FACT FILE

Fill in these Rock Facts as you learn about rocks in Chapter 3.

Igneous Rocks

Two types of igneous rock		
Colour		
Texture		
Other characteristics		
Where it can be found in Ireland		
Economic uses		

Sedimentary Rocks

Two types of sedimentary rock		
Colour		
Texture		
Other characteristics		
Where it can be found in Ireland		
Economic uses		

Metamorphic Rocks

Two types of metamorphic rock		
Colour		
Texture		
Other characteristics		
Where it can be found in Ireland		
Economic uses		

 KEY SKILLS

I used these two key skills during this portfolio activity:

SELF-ASSESSMENT

		Page	😊	😐	😞
1	I can list the ways in which rocks differ from each other.	39			
2	I know the three rock groups and I can explain how they are formed.	39			
3	I can name two types of igneous rock.	41			
4	I know how igneous rocks are formed and can give examples of where they are found in Ireland.	41			
5	I can name two types of sedimentary rock.	43			
6	I know how sedimentary rock is formed and can give examples of where it is found in Ireland.	43			
7	I can name two types of metamorphic rock.	44			
8	I know how metamorphic rock is formed and can give examples of where it is found in Ireland.	44			
9	I know how rocks can be used.	47			
10	I can explain the positive and negative socio-economic and environmental impacts of mining and quarrying.	47			

Write down examples of when you used the following Key Skills in this chapter:	
Being Literate	
Being Numerate	
Being Creative	
Managing Information and Thinking	
Working with Others	
Communicating	
Managing Myself	
Staying Well	

REFLECTION

List the Topics you know well here:

List the Topics you do not fully understand here:

List the Topics you have difficulty with here:

Write down your Revision Action Plan for this chapter here:

Rocks: How they are formed and used

Primary Economic Activities: How we use the world's natural resources

PORTFOLIO ACTIVITY 4.1: SUSTAINABLE DEVELOPMENT GOAL 6

PART 1

Read Matias's story on page 15 of this PDF: **https://educateplus.ie/go/goals**

List three issues that Matias has to deal with that you don't.

-

-

-

PART 2

Write a letter to your local TD asking them to support this Sustainable Development Goal and outlining why you think it is important.

 KEY SKILLS

I used these two key skills during this portfolio activity:

_____   _____

SELF-ASSESSMENT

		Page	🙂	😐	☹
1	I can list the three types of economic activity.	53			
2	I can explain the difference between renewable and non-renewable resources and give examples of each.	53			
3	I can explain the water cycle.	58			
4	I can explain how a local water supply works.	58			
5	I can explain the sustainable exploitation of water.	58			
6	I can explain what an irrigation scheme is.	58			
7	I understand how overfishing has occurred in Ireland.	61			
8	I understand the steps that have been taken to exploit fish sustainably in Ireland.	61			
9	I understand that farming is a system of inputs, outputs and processes.	64			
10	I can explain the different types of farm.	64			
11	I am aware that farming can have a negative impact on the environment and of the importance of sustainable farming.	64			
12	I understand how people have exploited wood over time.	66			
13	I am aware how important trees are in the prevention of climate change.	66			
14	I understand the steps taken in Ireland to reforest areas of land.	66			

Write down examples of when you used the following Key Skills in this chapter:	
Being Literate	
Being Numerate	
Being Creative	
Managing Information and Thinking	
Working with Others	
Communicating	
Managing Myself	
Staying Well	

REFLECTION

List the Topics you know well here:

List the Topics you do not fully understand here:

List the Topics you have difficulty with here:

Write down your Revision Action Plan for this chapter here:

Energy and the Environment: How fuelling our needs impacts on the world we live in

PORTFOLIO ACTIVITY 5.1: WIND – POSITIVE ENERGY FOR ALL!

We have learned about the advantages and disadvantages of wind farms.
*Go to **www.sliabhbawnwindfarm.ie** to see how a wind farm project in Strokestown, Co. Roscommon tried to work with the local community. Complete the template below.*

Location of site
Overview of project
Benefit to the environment
Benefit to the community
Recreation facilities

 KEY SKILLS

I used these two key skills during this portfolio activity:

_____   _____

PORTFOLIO ACTIVITY 5.2: GREENER SCHOOLS

Schools use a lot of energy every day. Discuss the following in groups of four:

1. How does your school use energy?

2. How could your school reduce the amount of energy it uses?

Share what you have learned by creating a poster for other students in your school.

Energy Saving Tips for Students

 KEY SKILLS

I used these two key skills during this portfolio activity:

_____   _____

Energy and the Environment: How fuelling our needs impacts on the world we live in

SELF-ASSESSMENT

		Page	☺	😐	☹
1	I can explain the differences between renewable and non-renewable energy resources and give examples of each.	71			
2	I can describe the different types of non-renewable resources.	76			
3	I understand the role non-renewable resources have to play in generating energy both in Ireland and abroad.	76			
4	I can identify non-renewable energy sources on Ordnance Survey maps.	76			
5	I can describe the different types of renewable energy resources.	79			
6	I can identify renewable energy resources on Ordnance Survey maps.	79			
7	I can explain how HEP and wind energy are produced in Ireland.	82			
8	I understand the positive and negative impacts of HEP and wind energy.	82			
9	I understand how our reliance on fossil fuels impacts the economy, environment and society.	85			
10	I can explain global warming, acid rain and smog.	85			

Write down examples of when you used the following Key Skills in this chapter:	
Being Literate	
Being Numerate	
Being Creative	
Managing Information and Thinking	
Working with Others	
Communicating	
Managing Myself	
Staying Well	

REFLECTION

REFLECTION

List the Topics you know well here:

List the Topics you do not fully understand here:

List the Topics you have difficulty with here:

Write down your Revision Action Plan for this chapter here:

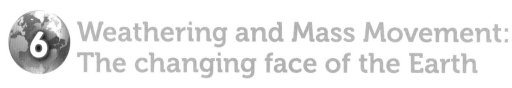

Weathering and Mass Movement: The changing face of the Earth

PORTFOLIO ACTIVITY 6.1: BURREN TOURISM AND SUSTAINABILITY

The Burren is a very delicate and unusual environment. It attracts numerous tourists each year to visit the region, bringing with them many environmental problems. The region has benefitted hugely from tourism but must be careful not to abuse the situation. Write a letter to your Principal outlining the reasons both for and against a school visit to the Burren. Use pictures to illustrate your points.

KEY SKILLS

I used these two key skills during this portfolio activity:

PORTFOLIO ACTIVITY 6.2: MASS MOVEMENT CASE STUDY

Type of mass movement _____

Where did it happen? (include a photograph or map of the area)	
When did it occur?	
Was this expected to happen in the region and has it happened before?	
What were the main causes of it occurring?	

List the negative environmental, social and economic impacts of the mass movement.	
What does the area look like now? (photographs can be included)	

 KEY SKILLS

I used these two key skills during this portfolio activity:

_____   _____

SELF-ASSESSMENT

		Page	🙂	😐	☹️
1	I can explain the difference between weathering and erosion.	91			
2	I can explain processes of mechanical weathering and chemical weathering.	91			
3	I can name and explain the formation of two surface features in a karst area.	97			
4	I can name and explain the formation of two underground features in a karst area.	97			
5	I can explain the link between this physical landscape and tourism.	97			
6	I can identify the links between tourism and the physical landscape on OS maps	97			
7	I can list and explain the factors that affect mass movement.	100			
8	I can name and explain examples of slow and fast mass movement.	100			
9	I understand the impact of mass movement on people.	100			
10	I understand the methods used to control mass movement.	100			

Write down examples of when you used the following Key Skills in this chapter:	
Being Literate	
Being Numerate	
Being Creative	
Managing Information and Thinking	
Working with Others	
Communicating	
Managing Myself	
Staying Well	

REFLECTION

List the Topics you know well here:

List the Topics you do not fully understand here:

List the Topics you have difficulty with here:

Write down your Revision Action Plan for this chapter here:

7 Geographical Skills for Second Years: Ordnance Survey and aerial photograph skills

SELF-ASSESSMENT

		Page	🙂	😐	🙁
1	I know how to measure distance and area on OS maps.	113			
2	I can identify various types of slope and draw a cross-section of an OS map.	113			
3	I can locate a suitable site for a residential area, shopping centre and factory on an OS map.	113			
4	I can identify the difference between vertical and oblique photographs.	120			
5	I can identify the time of year on an aerial photograph.	120			
6	I can identify the urban and rural functions on an aerial photograph.	120			
7	I can identify transport on an aerial photograph.	120			

Write down examples of when you used the following Key Skills in this chapter:	
Being Literate	
Being Numerate	
Being Creative	
Managing Information and Thinking	
Working with Others	
Communicating	
Managing Myself	
Staying Well	

REFLECTION

List the Topics you know well here:

List the Topics you do not fully understand here:

List the Topics you have difficulty with here:

Write down your Revision Action Plan for this chapter here:

8 Secondary Economic Activities: Industry in Ireland

PORTFOLIO ACTIVITY 8.1: STUDY OF A LOCAL INDUSTRY

Research a secondary economic activity in your area. It could be a multinational company or a small, local manufacturing plant like the furniture factory mentioned on page 123 of your textbook.

Name	
Location of industry	
What does it produce?	
Describe its function as a system.	
Why did it locate here?	
How many people does it employ?	
Are there many other businesses that benefit from the factory's location in the area?	
Does the community benefit in other ways than just employment?	
Are there any negative socio-economic impacts on the local people and community?	

 KEY SKILLS

I used these two key skills during this portfolio activity:

_____ _____

PORTFOLIO ACTIVITY 8.2: INDUSTRIAL DEVELOPMENT AND THE ENVIRONMENT

Divide into groups of eight and choose an example of when industrial development had implications for the environment.

Half the group (four students) should come up with arguments in favour of industrial development. The other half of the group should come up with arguments against industrial development. Don't forget to mention the environment during the debate.

Record the main points below and then perform the debate in front of the rest of the class.

In favour of industrial development	Against industrial development

 KEY SKILLS

I used these two key skills during this portfolio activity:

_____   _____

SELF-ASSESSMENT

		Page	🙂	😐	☹️
1	I understand what secondary economic activities are.	123			
2	I understand that secondary economic activities are a system of inputs, processes and outputs.	123			
3	I understand the factors that influence the location of a factory.	125			
4	I understand the different types of manufacturing industries.	131			
5	I can use Ordnance Survey maps to understand the location of industrial estates	131			
6	I understand why there is often conflict between industrial development and environmental issues.	132			

Write down examples of when you used the following Key Skills in this chapter:	
Being Literate	
Being Numerate	
Being Creative	
Managing Information and Thinking	
Working with Others	
Communicating	
Managing Myself	
Staying Well	

REFLECTION
REFLECTION

List the Topics you know well here:

List the Topics you do not fully understand here:

List the Topics you have difficulty with here:

Write down your Revision Action Plan for this chapter here:

9 Rivers: Shaping our landscape

PORTFOLIO ACTIVITY 9.1: FLOODING

Flooding is a natural disaster caused by the overflow of rivers due to heavy rainfall resulting in excess water in the river system. It can also occur because of people interfering with the river system. Flooding can have devastating effects on the landscape and can also have very negative socio-economic impacts.

Research a flood that has occurred locally, nationally or internationally and fill out the template below.

Date of flooding	
Location of flooding	River: Region/country: Village/town/city:
History of previous floods	
Cause of flooding	Weather: Human:
Responses to flooding	Local: National: International:
Short-term effects on the local people and the area	
Long-term effects on the local people and the area	
Plans put in place to reduce future flooding	

 **KEY SKILLS**

> I used these two key skills during this portfolio activity:
>
> _____   _____

PORTFOLIO ACTIVITY 9.2: RIVER SHANNON FAMILY HOLIDAY

You are planning a family cruise along the River Shannon. You have been put in charge of researching the holiday. Put together an itinerary for your family. Use the template below to help you.

Length of cruise:	
Starting point for cruise:	
End point for cruise:	
Size of group and their ages:	
Cost of boat hire:	
Sites to visit along the route:	
Activities:	
Places to moor (stay) at night:	
Cost of trip:	

Draw a map of your route. Fill in the distances between the places where you will moor at night. Mark the sites you plan to visit during your trip.

 KEY SKILLS

I used these two key skills during this portfolio activity:

_____   _____

Rivers: Shaping our landscape

SELF-ASSESSMENT

		Page	🙂	😐	☹️
1	I can explain the landforms that are commonly found along the route of a river.	138			
2	I can name and identify the three stages of a river.	138			
3	I understand the processes of river erosion, transportation and deposition.	140			
4	I can identify all landforms of erosion and deposition and I understand their formation in the youthful, mature and old stages of a river.	146			
5	I can explain in detail the formation of one landform of erosion.	146			
6	I can explain in detail the formation of one landform of deposition.	146			
7	I understand the different ways in which people interact with rivers.	150			
8	I have studied one negative and one positive way in which people interact with rivers.	150			
9	I can recognise river features and drainage features on an Ordnance Survey map.	153			

Write down examples of when you used the following Key Skills in this chapter:	
Being Literate	
Being Numerate	
Being Creative	
Managing Information and Thinking	
Working with Others	
Communicating	
Managing Myself	
Staying Well	

REFLECTION

List the Topics you know well here:

List the Topics you do not fully understand here:

List the Topics you have difficulty with here:

Write down your Revision Action Plan for this chapter here:

PORTFOLIO ACTIVITY 10.1: PEOPLE AND THE COAST

Many coastal areas are very dependent on tourism for their socio-economic development. However, this tourism has to be sustainable for both people and the environment. One such area is Doonbeg in Co. Clare. The golf resort at Doonbeg is famous all over the world. It is a links golf course, which means that it sits on sand dunes.

Your task is to research the reports from newspapers and online sources to give a detailed account of the problems facing Doonbeg golf course and its sand dunes, and the solution that has been offered. Complete the table below.

Problems facing the golf course	
Plan to protect the golf course	
Local impact on the environment	
Costs	
Importance of tourism to the region	
Local opinion on the project	
Outcome	
Do you think the decision was right and why?	

 KEY SKILLS

I used these two key skills during this portfolio activity:

_____   _____

PORTFOLIO ACTIVITY 10.2: COASTAL FLOODING

Flooding is a natural disaster that can happen along coastal areas due to severe storms or tectonic activity in the form of tsunamis. Flooding along coastal areas can have devastating effects on the landscape and can also have very negative socio-economic impacts.

Research a flood that has occurred locally, nationally or internationally and fill out the template below.

Date of flooding	
Location of flooding	Region/country: Village/town/city:
History of previous floods	
Cause of flooding	Weather: Tectonic activity:
Responses to flooding	Local: National: International:
Short-term effects on the local people and the area	
Long-term effects on the local people and the area	
Plans put in place to reduce future flooding	

 KEY SKILLS

I used these two key skills during this portfolio activity:

_____   _____

SELF-ASSESSMENT

		Page	😊	😐	☹️
1	I understand how waves are formed and the processes that help erode the coastline.	159			
2	I can identify features of coastal erosion.	163			
3	I can explain the formation of two features of coastal erosion.	163			
4	I can explain longshore drift.	167			
5	I can identify the features of coastal deposition.	167			
6	I can explain the formation of two features of coastal deposition.	167			
7	I can give examples of how people interact with the sea.	171			
8	I can explain, using examples, how people try to protect the coastline from erosion.	171			
9	I can recognise coastal landforms on an Ordnance Survey map.	172			

Write down examples of when you used the following Key Skills in this chapter:	
Being Literate	
Being Numerate	
Being Creative	
Managing Information and Thinking	
Working with Others	
Communicating	
Managing Myself	
Staying Well	

REFLECTION

List the Topics you know well here:

List the Topics you do not fully understand here:

List the Topics you have difficulty with here:

Write down your Revision Action Plan for this chapter here:

PORTFOLIO ACTIVITY 11.1: GLACIATION AND TOURISM (NATIONAL AND INTERNATIONAL)

Glacial landscapes are attractive to tourists for a number of reasons. The scenery is beautiful and there are many activities for tourists to enjoy, such as skiing, rock climbing, hiking, mountain biking and hang gliding.

Tourism as an economic activity brings advantages and disadvantages for the local communities that live in the region.

Research an area where there is a glacial landscape. Find out what activities are already in place and assess the potential for further development. You could pick Glendalough or the Glen of the Downs in Co. Wicklow, the Gap of Dunloe in Co. Kerry or the drumlin landscape of Clew Bay in Co. Mayo for example. You could also pick an international example, such as the Chamonix ski area in France, Franz Josef Glacier in New Zealand or Glacier National Park in Montana, USA. You can also choose your own example.

Area of study	Region/country: Village/town/city:
Glacial features found there	
Tourism developments to date	

Potential for tourism in the future	
Positive impacts of tourism on the area	
Negative impacts of tourism on the area	

 KEY SKILLS

I used these two key skills during this portfolio activity:

_____   _____

SELF-ASSESSMENT

		Page	🙂	😐	☹️
1	I understand some of the reasons why ice ages may occur.	180			
2	I can explain the two processes of glacial erosion.	180			
3	I can identify landforms of glacial erosion.	183			
4	I can explain the formation of two landforms of glacial erosion.	183			
5	I can explain how glaciers transport their load.	187			
6	I can identify landforms of glacial deposition and fluvio-glacial deposition.	187			
7	I can explain the formation of two landforms of glacial deposition and two landforms of fluvio-glacial deposition.	187			
8	I can explain the positive and negative influences of glaciation on human activity.	189			
9	I can recognise landforms of glaciation on an Ordnance Survey map.	191			

Write down examples of when you used the following Key Skills in this chapter:	
Being Literate	
Being Numerate	
Being Creative	
Managing Information and Thinking	
Working with Others	
Communicating	
Managing Myself	
Staying Well	

REFLECTION

List the Topics you know well here:

List the Topics you do not fully understand here:

List the Topics you have difficulty with here:

Write down your Revision Action Plan for this chapter here:

Glaciation: The work of ice

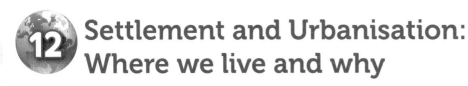

12 Settlement and Urbanisation: Where we live and why

PORTFOLIO ACTIVITY 12.1: SUSTAINABLE RURAL DEVELOPMENT

Some people argue that rural settlements are unsustainable. You may have seen in the news that Garda stations, post offices and bus routes in some rural areas have been closed down.

Imagine you are the Taoiseach. What would you do to attract more people to rural areas and to cater for the existing communities? Make a list below and then present your ideas to your class. Vote for the best ideas.

How to attract more people to rural areas	How to cater for existing communities

 KEY SKILLS

I used these two key skills during this portfolio activity:

_____   _____

PORTFOLIO ACTIVITY 12.2: URBAN RENEWAL/REDEVELOPMENT

Find an area in your local town or city that has undergone urban renewal or redevelopment. Write a brief description of the area with your class and teacher. Describe what happened to the area and what existed before the redevelopment or renewal.

Name of area	
Description of the area	
Renewal or redevelopment	
What existed before?	
What is present now?	
How would you have improved this urban renewal/ redevelopment?	

 KEY SKILLS

I used these two key skills during this portfolio activity:

_____

SELF-ASSESSMENT

		Page	🙂	😐	🙁
1	I understand how site and situation have affected settlement.	200			
2	I can identify site and situation factors on an Ordnance Survey map.	200			
3	I understand the different time periods of historic settlement in Ireland.	203			
4	I can identify those settlements on an Ordnance Survey map.	203			
5	I understand what a function of a settlement is.	208			
6	I understand that settlements can have multiple functions and that the functions of settlements can change over time.	208			
7	I can identify functions of settlements on an OS map and an aerial photograph.	208			
8	I can explain the rural patterns of settlement in Ireland today.	209			
9	I can identify rural patterns of settlement on Ordnance Survey maps.	209			
10	I can explain what urbanisation is and the problems associated with urbanisation.	212			
11	I can give examples of solutions to the problems associated with urbanisation.	216			
12	I know what the different functional zones in cities are.	221			
13	I can explain how land value is linked to land use.	221			
14	I can recognise different types of housing in urban areas.	221			
15	I understand what a primate city it.	221			

Write down examples of when you used the following Key Skills in this chapter:	
Being Literate	
Being Numerate	
Being Creative	
Managing Information and Thinking	
Working with Others	
Communicating	
Managing Myself	
Staying Well	

REFLECTION

REFLECTION

List the Topics you know well here:

List the Topics you do not fully understand here:

List the Topics you have difficulty with here:

Write down your Revision Action Plan for this chapter here:

Settlement and Urbanisation: Where we live and why

13 Weather: How it impacts on our lives

PORTFOLIO ACTIVITY 13.1: MAKE YOUR OWN WEATHER STATION!

Set up a weather station in your school with your classmates.

Does your school have access to any weather instruments? If not, you can always make your own. You will find useful tips on the following websites:

- **https://educateplus.ie/go/weather-station**
- **https://educateplus.ie/go/weather-station-2**

Remember to keep your weather station in an open and unsheltered area. Record the data on a daily basis for a week to start with and illustrate your information on graphs.

Your class, year group or school can then try to keep track of this information over the course of a month or even a term.

	Monday	Tuesday	Wednesday	Thursday	Friday
Precipitation					
Temperature					
Wind direction					
Wind speed					
Humidity					
Sunshine					
Atmospheric pressure					

1. Draw a line graph to represent the level of rainfall and temperatures for the week.

2. Draw a bar chart to show wind speed for the week.

3. Draw a pie chart to show the hours of sunshine for the week.

KEY SKILLS

I used these two key skills during this portfolio activity:

_____   _____

PORTFOLIO ACTIVITY 13.2: REPORT ON EX-HURRICANE OPHELIA

In October 2017, ex-hurricane Ophelia hit Ireland. It was the first time in history that a hurricane like this had made landfall in Ireland. For this activity you must research Ophelia and put together a newspaper report on the event. Include photographs/pictures and mention the following:

- Hurricane details (wind speed, charts, travel path, etc.)
- Warnings issued and actions taken by the government
- Damage caused and death toll
- Reaction of people to the hurricane (interview someone who experienced the hurricane)
- Aftermath and clean-up operation
- Was the reaction to the natural disaster sufficient and well planned?

Headline _____

Reporter's name _____

KEY SKILLS

I used these two key skills during this portfolio activity:

SELF-ASSESSMENT

		Page	☺	😐	☹
1	I understand that the Earth's atmosphere is made up of gases.	227			
2	I can name the layers of the atmosphere.	227			
3	I can explain the distribution of solar energy over the Earth's surface and within the atmosphere.	229			
4	I can explain the Earth's orbit around the Sun.	229			
5	I understand how the unequal heating of the Earth's surface leads to the movement of wind.	230			
6	I understand the main global winds.	230			
7	I understand the heating of the Earth's surface and how it results in ocean currents.	231			
8	I understand air masses and how they form fronts.	235			
9	I can explain the different fronts that are formed and I can identify them on weather maps.	235			
10	I understand how clouds form and I can identify the various types of clouds.	237			
11	I understand how rain forms.	238			
12	I can explain convectional rain, cyclonic rain and relief rain.	238			
13	I can list the instruments used to measure different aspects of weather and the units they are measured in.	246			
14	I can explain the formation and impact of a serious weather disaster.	246			

Write down examples of when you used the following Key Skills in this chapter:	
Being Literate	
Being Numerate	
Being Creative	
Managing Information and Thinking	
Working with Others	
Communicating	
Managing Myself	
Staying Well	

REFLECTION

List the Topics you know well here:

List the Topics you do not fully understand here:

List the Topics you have difficulty with here:

Write down your Revision Action Plan for this chapter here:

14 Climates: Classifying climate types and Ireland's climate

PORTFOLIO ACTIVITY 14.1: RESEARCH A CLIMATE

You have learned that there are three broad climatic zones in the world and you have learned about the main characteristics of each.

Choose a climate and research it. Fill in the table below.

Name of climate	
Location	
Average summer temperature	
Average winter temperature	
Precipitation	
Soil type	
Natural vegetation	
Wildlife	
Human activity	

KEY SKILLS

I used these two key skills during this portfolio activity:

_____   _____

PORTFOLIO ACTIVITY 14.2: CLIMATE CHANGE – WHAT CAN WE DO?

Global warming is one of the most worrying environmental problems of our time. Discuss strategies with your classmates on what you can do to help stop global warming. Draw up a class charter with five changes you and your classmates are going to make to try to reduce your impact on the causes of climate change.

1.	
2.	
3.	
4.	
5.	

KEY SKILLS

I used these two key skills during this portfolio activity:

_____   _____

Climates: Classifying climate types and Ireland's climate

SELF-ASSESSMENT

		Page	🙂	😐	🙁
1	I can explain what climate is.	255			
2	I can explain the three factors that influence global climates.	255			
3	I can explain the two factors that influence climate locally.	255			
4	I can give examples of hot climates, temperate climates and cold climates.	260			
5	I can outline the main characteristics of each global climate type.	260			
6	I can explain the factors that influence Ireland's climate.	261			
7	I understand the causes and implications of climate change.	266			
8	I can explain what is being done to tackle climate change.	266			

Write down examples of when you used the following Key Skills in this chapter:	
Being Literate	
Being Numerate	
Being Creative	
Managing Information and Thinking	
Working with Others	
Communicating	
Managing Myself	
Staying Well	

REFLECTION

List the Topics you know well here:

List the Topics you do not fully understand here:

List the Topics you have difficulty with here:

Write down your Revision Action Plan for this chapter here:

SELF-ASSESSMENT

		Page	😊	😐	😞
1.	I understand the key differences and similarities between OS maps and aerial photographs.	274			
2	I can identify the direction a camera was facing for an aerial photograph using an OS map.	274			
3	I can draw a sketch map of an aerial photograph.	280			
4	I know how to interpret satellite imagery.	283			

Write down examples of when you used the following Key Skills in this chapter:	
Being Literate	
Being Numerate	
Being Creative	
Managing Information and Thinking	
Working with Others	
Communicating	
Managing Myself	
Staying Well	

REFLECTION

List the Topics you know well here:

List the Topics you do not fully understand here:

List the Topics you have difficulty with here:

Write down your Revision Action Plan for this chapter here:

16 Soil: A vital natural resource

PORTFOLIO ACTIVITY 16.1: SOIL INVESTIGATION

Collect a jar of soil from your local area. It is important to dig down at least 15 cm when you are collecting your sample. Record information about your soil sample in the table below:

My Soil Sample

Photograph of the jar with sample soil	
What colour is the soil?	
What location did you get the soil from?	

Soil: A vital natural resource

What is the soil used for? / What is growing there?	
Describe the texture of the soil.	
What is the pH level of the soil?	
What type of soil do you think it is?	
What would grow well in this soil?	

 KEY SKILLS

I used these two key skills during this portfolio activity:

_____ _____

SELF-ASSESSMENT

		Page	🙂	😐	🙁
1	I can explain what the five ingredients of soil are.	287			
2	I understand what soil texture is.	287			
3	I can draw and label a soil profile.	287			
4	I can explain leaching.	287			
5	I understand the factors that lead to soil formation.	289			
6	I understand the various types of soil found in Ireland.	292			
7	I understand how soil and vegetation influence each other.	294			
8	I can explain the impact humans have on soil.	299			
9	I understand the need for sustainable exploitation of soil.	299			

Write down examples of when you used the following Key Skills in this chapter:	
Being Literate	
Being Numerate	
Being Creative	
Managing Information and Thinking	
Working with Others	
Communicating	
Managing Myself	
Staying Well	

REFLECTION

List the Topics you know well here:

List the Topics you do not fully understand here:

List the Topics you have difficulty with here:

Write down your Revision Action Plan for this chapter here:

Soil: A vital natural resource

17 Tertiary Economic Activities: Transport and tourism

PORTFOLIO ACTIVITY 17.1: TOURISM CASE STUDY

Research two tourist destinations, one in Ireland and one abroad. Fill out the fact sheets below.

Tourist region in Ireland	
Physical World	
Climate	
Landscape detail (beaches, scenery, etc.)	
Attraction	
Activities	
Tours	
Transport	
How to get there (give details on how to get there, i.e. flights, ferry, car, rail, etc.)	
How to get around when there (public transport, car rental, bikes, etc.)	
Impact	
Positive impacts of tourism for the region (e.g. employment/improved services)	
Negative impacts of tourism for the region (e.g. pollution, altering physical landscape, impact on locals)	

Tourist region abroad	
Physical World	
Climate	
Landscape detail (beaches, scenery, etc.)	
Attraction	
Activities	
Tours	
Transport	
How to get there (give details on how to get there, i.e. flights, ferry, car, rail, etc.)	
How to get around when there (public transport, car rental, bikes, etc.)	
Impact	
Positive impacts of tourism for the region (e.g. employment/improved services)	
Negative impacts of tourism for the region (e.g. pollution, altering physical landscape, impact on locals)	

KEY SKILLS

I used these two key skills during this portfolio activity:

_____ _____

SELF-ASSESSMENT

		Page	🙂	😐	☹️
1	I understand the importance of tourism to Ireland and Europe.	307			
2	I understand that tourism, transport and the physical world are all interrelated.	311			
3	I understand how the physical landscape influences tourism in Ireland and the impact tourism has on the physical landscape as a result.	311			
4	I understand the importance of sustainable tourism.	311			
5	I understand how tourism influences transport.	311			
6	I understand that tourism, transport and the physical world are all interrelated.	315			
7	I understand how Ireland's transport network has developed.	315			
8	I understand the influence of the physical landscape on transport and the influence transport has on the physical world.	315			
9	I understand how transport influences tourism.	315			
10	I can recognise tertiary economic activities on Ordnance Survey maps.	317			
11	I can identify the links between the physical world, transport and tourism on Ordnance Survey maps.	317			

Write down examples of when you used the following Key Skills in this chapter:	
Being Literate	
Being Numerate	
Being Creative	
Managing Information and Thinking	
Working with Others	
Communicating	
Managing Myself	
Staying Well	

REFLECTION

REFLECTION

List the Topics you know well here:

List the Topics you do not fully understand here:

List the Topics you have difficulty with here:

Write down your Revision Action Plan for this chapter here:

18 Population: How population changes over time

PORTFOLIO ACTIVITY 18.1: POPULATION GROWTH IN YOUR LOCAL AREA

Imagine your local area is expected to experience high levels of population growth in the next 25 years. How could your local area prepare for any potential problems?

Divide into groups of four, share your ideas and then complete the table below.

The first topic has been partly completed for you.

Topic	Potential Problem	Solution
Housing	<ul><li>Shortage of housing for residents</li><li>Lack of open spaces on which to build residential developments</li></ul>	<ul><li>Development of current derelict sites for housing</li><li>Change from building houses to apartment blocks to save space</li></ul>
Schools		
Employment opportunities		
Traffic		

Hospitals		
Waste and water supply		
Childcare		
Other		

KEY SKILLS

I used these two key skills during this portfolio activity:

_____   _____

SELF-ASSESSMENT

		Page	😊	😐	😞
1	I understand why populations change.	324			
2	I can calculate whether a population is increasing or decreasing.	324			
3	I understand the factors that lead to population growth in developed and developing countries.	328			
4	I understand the demographic transition model.	330			
5	I understand the different views of population growth in the future.	330			
6	I know how to read population pyramids.	332			
7	I understand how population pyramids can be used to plan for the future.	332			
8	I can explain how and why Ireland's population has changed over the years.	335			
9	I can explain how and why the population of a developing world country has changed.	335			

Write down examples of when you used the following Key Skills in this chapter:	
Being Literate	
Being Numerate	
Being Creative	
Managing Information and Thinking	
Working with Others	
Communicating	
Managing Myself	
Staying Well	

REFLECTION

REFLECTION

List the Topics you know well here:

List the Topics you do not fully understand here:

List the Topics you have difficulty with here:

Write down your Revision Action Plan for this chapter here:

19 Migration: People on the move

PORTFOLIO ACTIVITY 19.1: REPORT ON A REFUGEE CAMP

There are a lot of stories in the news today about migration. There are refugee camps in many places in Europe such as in Greece and in Calais in France. Research one of these refugee camps and write a report. You could include the following:

● Where are the refugees from?

● Why did they have to flee their country?

● What are the conditions like in the refugee camp?

● What are European countries doing to help these refugees?

_____

_____

_____

_____

_____

_____

_____

_____

_____

_____

_____

_____

_____

_____

_____

_____

_____

_____

 KEY SKILLS

I used these two key skills during this portfolio activity:

_____   _____

PORTFOLIO ACTIVITY 19.2: MIGRATION IN MY FAMILY

Interview a family member who has migrated for one reason or another. It could be someone who was born in another area of Ireland and relocated or it could be someone who now lives in another country or used to live in another country.

Here are some questions you might ask:

- Where and when were you born?
- What was life like when you were growing up?
- What was school like?
- Did you go to university?
- What activities did you enjoy?
- What were the push factors that made you leave?
- What were the pull factors that made you choose the place to which you moved?

Question _____

Answer _____

_____

_____

Question _____

Answer _____

_____

_____

Question _____

Answer _____

_____

_____

Question _____

Answer _____

_____

_____

Question _____

Answer _____

_____

_____

Question _____

Answer _____

_____

_____

_____

Question _____

Answer _____

_____

_____

_____

Question _____

Answer _____

_____

_____

_____

Question _____

Answer _____

_____

_____

_____

 **KEY SKILLS**

I used these two key skills during this portfolio activity:

_____ _____

Migration: People on the move

SELF-ASSESSMENT

		Page	😊	😐	😞
1	I understand what migration is.	347			
2	I can explain the causes of migration (push and pull factors).	347			
3	I can explain the barriers that can stop migration.	347			
4	I can explain the consequences of migration.	347			
5	I can explain the causes and consequences of organised migration.	349			

Write down examples of when you used the following Key Skills in this chapter:

Being Literate	
Being Numerate	
Being Creative	
Managing Information and Thinking	
Working with Others	
Communicating	
Managing Myself	
Staying Well	

REFLECTION

REFLECTION

List the Topics you know well here:

List the Topics you do not fully understand here:

List the Topics you have difficulty with here:

Write down your Revision Action Plan for this chapter here:

PORTFOLIO ACTIVITY 20.1: SPEECH ON IRELAND AND AID

There is a saying, 'Charity begins at home'. Some people argue that Ireland should deal with problems at home such as homelessness, unemployment and crime rather than sending money to the developing world.

Write a short speech on why Ireland should continue to support its overseas development assistance programme through Irish Aid and NGOs. Research some of the success stories of Irish Aid or an Irish NGO for your speech.

Economic Inequality: A world divided

 KEY SKILLS

I used these two key skills during this portfolio activity:

_____

PORTFOLIO ACTIVITY 20.2: SUSTAINABLE DEVELOPMENT GOALS

Examine all of the Sustainable Development Goals at **https://educateplus.ie/go/dev-goals.**

Choose a goal that deals with inequality in the world. Design an information sheet about this goal.

Use the following points to help you brainstorm ideas:

- Why you think this goal is important
- Three facts about this goal
- Three things we can do to achieve this goal

Goal

Three facts

Three things we can do

KEY SKILLS

I used these two key skills during this portfolio activity:

_____   _____

SELF-ASSESSMENT

		Page	🙂	😐	🙁
1	I can classify countries into different groups according to their economic development.	356			
2	I understand that there are different methods of measuring economic development.	356			
3	I understand that inequality exists between the developing and developed worlds.	361			
4	I understand the reasons why inequality exists and can give some possible solutions.	361			
5	I can explain the different types of aid.	364			
6	I can give examples of Ireland's overseas aid programmes.	364			
7	I can explain the positive and negative impacts of aid.	364			
8	I can explain how my life chances differ from those of a young person in the developing world.	368			

Write down examples of when you used the following Key Skills in this chapter:	
Being Literate	
Being Numerate	
Being Creative	
Managing Information and Thinking	
Working with Others	
Communicating	
Managing Myself	
Staying Well	

REFLECTION

REFLECTION

List the Topics you know well here:

List the Topics you do not fully understand here:

List the Topics you have difficulty with here:

Write down your Revision Action Plan for this chapter here:

Economic Inequality: A world divided

21 Globalisation: Living in an interconnected world

PORTFOLIO ACTIVITY 21.1: GLOBALISATION AND MUSIC

Design a poster that shows the connections between the music you listen to and the rest of the world.

Use the following questions to help you brainstorm ideas:

- What is the nationality of the singer/band of the most recent song that you listened to?
- What technology do you most commonly use to listen to music?
- Where is the technology made?
- Where is the company that owns the technology based?
- Where and how did you buy the technology (online purchases or physically bought from retail outlets)?

KEY SKILLS

I used these two key skills during this portfolio activity:

_____   _____

PORTFOLIO ACTIVITY 21.2: FOR OR AGAINST GLOBALISATION?

Globalisation is one of the most interesting yet controversial topics of this generation. Below is a plus, minus and interesting chart (PMI Chart). Using what you have learned in this chapter, fill in the chart.

P	M	I

 Are you for or against globalisation? Discuss your findings with the class.

 KEY SKILLS

I used these two key skills during this portfolio activity:

_____   _____

Globalisation: Living in an interconnected world

SELF-ASSESSMENT

		Page	😊	😐	☹️
1	I understand what globalisation is.	376			
2	I understand the factors that influence globalisation.	376			
3	I can explain how globalisation impacts on people all over the world.	378			
4	I can evaluate how globalisation is interlinked with population, settlement and human development.	381			
5	I can discuss the possible future of globalisation.	381			

Write down examples of when you used the following Key Skills in this chapter:	
Being Literate	
Being Numerate	
Being Creative	
Managing Information and Thinking	
Working with Others	
Communicating	
Managing Myself	
Staying Well	

REFLECTION

List the Topics you know well here:

List the Topics you do not fully understand here:

List the Topics you have difficulty with here:

Write down your Revision Action Plan for this chapter here:

New Geography in Action

Junior Cycle Geography

Activity Book

Norma Lenihan & Jason O'Brien

educate.ie

PUBLISHED BY:

Educate.ie
Walsh Educational Books Ltd
Castleisland, Co. Kerry, Ireland
www.educate.ie

PRINTED AND BOUND BY:

Walsh Colour Print
Castleisland, Co. Kerry, Ireland

ISBN: 978-1-912239-42-9

ACKNOWLEDGEMENTS

For permission to reproduce artwork, the authors and publisher acknowledge the following copyright holders:
© ALAMY LTD: Carolyn Jenkins / Alamy Stock Photo 47; Adrian Turner / Alamy Stock Photo 49 (sea wall); Pam Biddle / Alamy Stock Photo 49 (gabion); Alexey Solodov / Alamy Stock Photo 66TL · © BARROW/COAKLEY PHOTOGRAPHY: 29, 62B · © BIGSTOCK IMAGES: Speedfighter / Bigstock 49 (rock armour); presian1801 / Bigstock 62TL; mbtaichi / Bigstock 62TR; longlens / Bigstock 62CL; SuperlightR / Bigstock 62CR; neillang / Bigstock 66CL; PaulMaguire / Bigstock 66TR · © GETTY IMAGES INC: German Aeorpace Center DLR/ZKI via Getty Images 79 (D) · © GOOGLE EARTH: 76 (all), 77 (all), 79 (B, C) · © JOHN HERRIOTT PHOTOGRAPHY: 74, 84 · © NASA: 78 (all), 79 (A) · © ORDNANCE SURVEY OF IRELAND: 2, 28, 57, 58 (all), 75, 80 · © SHUTTERSTOCK INC: SADLERC1 / Shutterstock 49 (groynes); Darryl Sleath / Shutterstock 68 (barograph); Sarah Camille / Shutterstock 68 (anemometer); 501room / Shutterstock 68 (Campbell-Stokes recorder).

Ordnance Survey Ireland Permit No. 9153
© Ordnance Survey Ireland/Government of Ireland

Activity Book
Contents

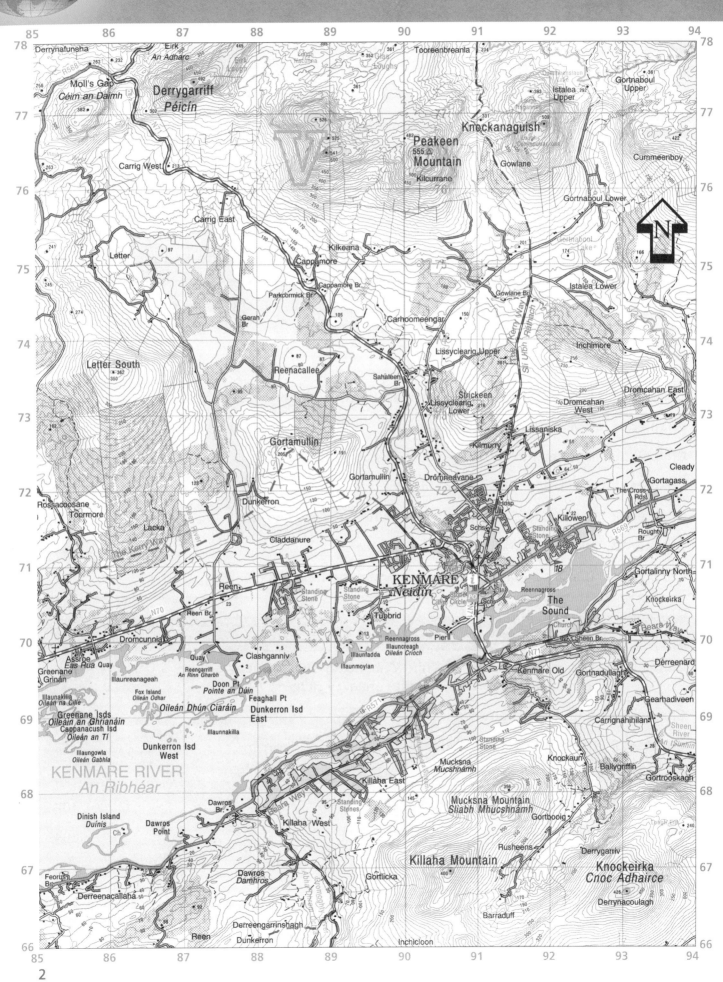

Examine the OS map of Kenmare opposite and answer these questions.

1. Draw a sketch map of the Kenmare OS map and include the following:

(a) Urban area of Kenmare   (c) Beara Way walkway   (e) An upland area over 200 m

(b) N70 and N71   (d) The dismantled railway line

2. Name the following:

(a) The mountain range at V 90 76 _____

(b) The Gap located at V 85 77 _____

(c) The townland at V 92 74 _____

3. Give the four-figure grid reference for the following:

(a) An 18-hole golf course _____

(b) An area of coniferous woodland _____

(c) The townland area of Dromcahan East _____

4. What antiquities are located at the following six-figure grid references?

(a) V 884 705 _____

(b) V 926 748 _____

(c) V 922 703 _____

3

5. Give the six-figure grid reference for the following on the map:

(a) Caravan park _____

(b) Post office in Kenmare Town _____

(c) Triangulation pillar on Peakeen Mountain _____

6. What direction would you be travelling:

(a) if you left Kenmare and cycled along the Ring of Kerry cycle route on the N70 towards Greenane? _____

(b) if you left Kenmare and cycled along the Ring of Kerry cycle route towards Moll Gap on the N71? _____

(c) if you were walking from Kenmare along the Kerry Way walkway towards Peakeen Mountain? _____

7. List **four** ways height is shown on OS maps. Use examples and locations from the Kenmare Ordnance Survey map.

(a) _____

(b) _____

(c) _____

(d) _____

8.

Month	Jan	Feb	Mar	Apr	May	Jun	Jul	Aug	Sep	Oct	Nov	Dec
Temperature (°C)	5.8	6.6	7.9	6.7	10.5	13.0	13.9	15.4	11.8	8.0	5.5	2.9
Precipitation (mm)	97.4	42.4	15.4	75.4	55.1	175.1	122.1	129.1	62.0	90.9	68.3	25.4

Examine the table above showing the mean monthly temperature and precipitation levels in Mullingar in 2015.

(a) Draw a bar chart illustrating the temperatures for the year in Mullingar in 2015.

(b) Draw a trend graph illustrating both the temperatures and the precipitation levels for the first six months of the year (January to June).

9. Look at the following information and draw a pie chart to illustrate the data.

Energy Use in the Home

Energy Use	% Usage
Heating rooms	60%
Hot water	24%
Electrical appliances	7%
Lighting	6%
Cooking	3%

Geographical Skills for First Years: Ordnance Survey and graph skills

1. Label the diagram.

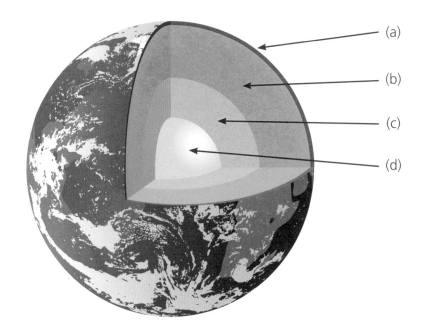

(a) _____

(b) _____

(c) _____

(d) _____

2. Define the following terms:

(a) Core

_____

_____

_____

(b) Mantle

_____

_____

_____

(c) Crust

_____

_____

_____

3. How do convection currents work and how do they make the plates move?

_____

_____

_____

_____

_____

4. Name the plates in the diagram.

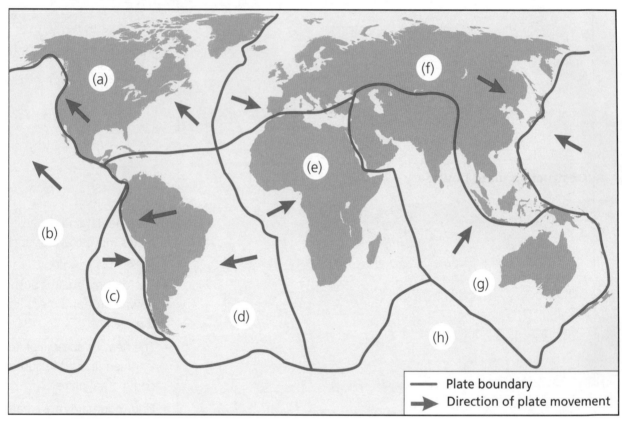

(a) _____

(b) _____

(c) _____

(d) _____

(e) _____

(f) _____

(g) _____

(h) _____

5. Draw diagrams in the boxes below to show the following three plate boundaries. Use the sentences beside them to label your diagrams.

Constructive plate boundary

- Molten magma rises through the mantle to the surface
- The two plates move apart from each other, leaving a gap
- Lava creates new crust
- Mid-ocean ridges are formed

Destructive plate boundary

- Continental and oceanic plates move towards each other
- The oceanic crust is pushed downwards and melts into the mantle
- The heavier oceanic plate is forced under the lighter continental plate
- Fold mountains are created

Passive plate boundary

- Two plates are sliding past each other
- An earthquake happens here
- The tectonic plates are moving at different speeds in the same direction

6. Using your diagrams opposite, write a detailed description of the three plate boundaries below.

Constructive plate boundaries

_____

_____

_____

_____

_____

_____

_____

_____

Destructive plate boundaries

_____

_____

_____

_____

_____

_____

_____

_____

Passive plate boundaries

_____

_____

_____

_____

_____

_____

_____

_____

_____

7. Draw a labelled diagram of a volcano using the following terms:

- Vent
- Crater
- Magma chamber
- Volcanic cone
- Ash cloud
- Layers of lava

8. List the **three** different types of volcano that can be found on the Earth's surface.

(a) _____

(b) _____

(c) _____

9. Name a volcano that you have studied and explain **one** positive and **one** negative socio-economic effect.

_____

_____

_____

_____

_____

10. Label the diagram below.

_____

_____

_____

_____

11. Match the terms with the descriptions of them.

1.	Richter scale	**A.**	A possible consequence of an earthquake that happens under the sea
2.	Focus	**B.**	Smaller earthquakes after the main one
3.	Epicentre	**C.**	The point on the Earth's surface above the focus
4.	Aftershocks	**D.**	The scale used to measure the strength of earthquakes
5.	Tsunami	**E.**	The place in the Earth's crust where an earthquake occurs

1. _____   **2.** _____   **3.** _____   **4.** _____   **5.** _____

12. The following sentences describing how an earthquake occurs are in the wrong order. Put them in the correct order by numbering them 1 to 5.

This pressure is suddenly released in a jerky movement.	
Earthquakes occur at plate margins.	
The plates sometimes lock, causing pressure to build.	
This release of pressure is called an earthquake.	
As the plates move past each other at the margins, the movement is not smooth.	

13. List **three** results of an earthquake occurring in a region.

(a) _____

(b) _____

(c) _____

14. Name the **three** types of fold mountains found on the Earth's surface.

(a) _____

(b) _____

(c) _____

15. Give **two** examples of fold mountains formed in Ireland during the Armorican period.

(a) _____

(b) _____

1. List **three** ways in which rocks differ from one another.

    (a) _____

    (b) _____

    (c) _____

2. Name a county in which each of these rock types can be found.

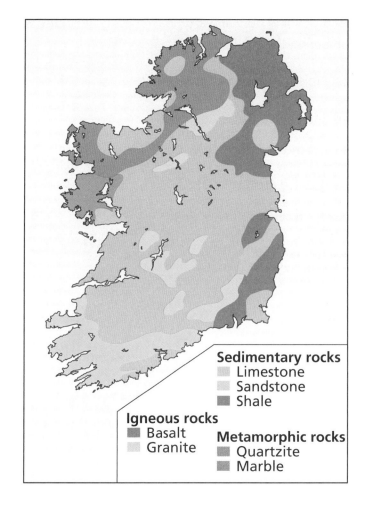

Sedimentary rocks
- Limestone
- Sandstone
- Shale

Igneous rocks
- Basalt
- Granite

Metamorphic rocks
- Quartzite
- Marble

    (a) Basalt: _____

    (b) Granite: _____

    (c) Limestone: _____

    (d) Sandstone: _____

    (e) Shale: _____

    (f) Quartzite: _____

    (g) Marble: _____

3. Label the diagram below.

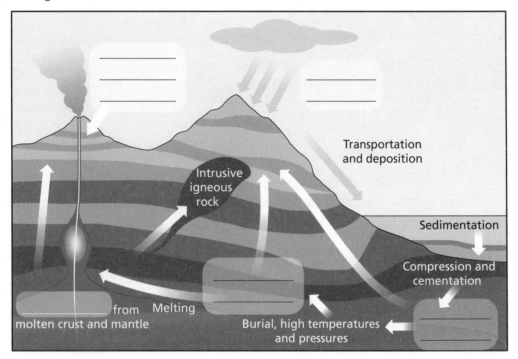

4. Which rock type (igneous, metamorphic or sedimentary) matches each fact below?

	They are formed as a result of volcanic activity. Hot molten magma escapes from the mantle.
	They are formed from particles of rock and dead plants and animals.
	They are formed from rocks that already exist.
	It cools and solidifies quickly on the Earth's surface or slowly deep inside the crust.
	Layers of this material build up over time and are compressed and cemented to create solid rock.
	They form when igneous or sedimentary rocks are changed into new, harder rocks by great heat or pressure or both.

5. Name an igneous rock of your choice and describe in detail how it is formed, giving an example of its location in Ireland.

Name: _____

Formation: _____

_____

_____

Example in Ireland: _____

6. Name a sedimentary rock of your choice and describe in detail how it is formed, giving an example of its location in Ireland

   Name: _____

   Formation: _____

   _____

   _____

   Example in Ireland: _____

7. Name a metamorphic rock of your choice and describe in detail how it is formed, giving an example of its location in Ireland.

   Name: _____

   Formation: _____

   _____

   _____

   Example in Ireland: _____

8. In the table below fill in some information regarding human activities and rocks.

   List **two** positive and **two** negative socio-economic impacts of quarrying and mining in a local community.

Positive	Negative
(a)	(a)
(b)	(b)

4 Primary Economic Activities:
How we use the world's natural resources

1. Define the following terms:

(a) Economic activities

_____

_____

(b) Primary economic activities

_____

_____

(c) Secondary economic activities

_____

_____

(d) Tertiary economic activities

_____

_____

(e) Natural resources

_____

_____

(f) Renewable resources

_____

_____

(g) Non-renewable resources

_____

_____

2. Add these labels to the diagram:

(a) Evaporation

(b) Condensation

(c) Precipitation

(d) Run off

3. Local water supply

Name a local water supply you have studied.	
What river does the water come from?	
How much water is supplied each day?	
Why is filtering used?	
Explain why chemicals are added to the water. Name two of these chemicals.	
Where is the water then stored?	
How does the water get to our taps?	

4. Irrigation schemes

Name an irrigation scheme you have studied.	
Why was an irrigation scheme needed in this area?	
Describe the stages of building this irrigation scheme.	
Explain two advantages of this scheme.	
Explain two disadvantages of this scheme.	

5. Describe and explain **three** reasons for overfishing.

(a) _____

_____

_____

(b) _____

_____

_____

(c) _____

_____

_____

6. Describe and explain **three** measures taken to limit the amount of fish being caught.

(a) _____

_____

(b) _____

_____

(c) _____

_____

7. What is meant by sustainable fishing?

_____

_____

_____

8. Define the following:

(a) Potable water _____

_____

(b) Depletion _____

_____

(c) Irrigation _____

_____

(d) Sustainable exploitation _____

_____

9. Look at the following words and write input, output or process beside each one. Give a reason for each answer.

	Input/Process/Output	Reason
Vegetables		
Cow		
Ploughing		
Machinery		
Harvesting		
Milk		

10. Link the following farm types to the correct produce.

Dairy	grazing sheep
Arable	flowers
Horticulture	cows
Pastoral	pigs
Livestock	wheat

11. Describe **two** negative impacts of farming on the environment.

_____

_____

_____

_____

_____

_____

12. Explain **two** ways in which farmers can help develop sustainable farming.

_____

_____

_____

_____

_____

_____

13. Why in recent years has there been an increase in the development of forestry in Ireland? Give **two** reasons for your answer.

_____

_____

_____

_____

14. Draw a suitable graph to display the information on forestry ownership in Ireland in the table below:

Ownership	Area (ha)	%
Public	395,760	54.1
Private (grant aided)	246,550	33.7
Private (other)	89,350	12.2
Total	**731,650**	**100**

Source: NFI, 2012

5 Energy and the Environment:
How fuelling our needs impacts on the world we live in

1. What are natural resources?

_____

_____

2. Define the word finite.

_____

_____

3. Define the word infinite.

_____

_____

4. List **three** renewable energy sources that we use in Ireland.

(a) _____

(b) _____

(c) _____

5. Explain **two** benefits of using renewable energy.

_____

_____

_____

_____

6. State **two** positives and **two** negatives of wind energy production in Ireland.

Positive	Negative
(a)	(a)
(b)	(b)

7. State **two** positives and **two** negatives of HEP production in Ireland.

Positive	Negative
(a)	(a)
(b)	(b)

8. List **three** non-renewable resources we use in Ireland.

(a) _____

(b) _____

(c) _____

9. Explain **two** negative impacts of using non-renewable energy.

_____

_____

_____

_____

10. Draw a labelled diagram showing how acid rain occurs.

11. List and explain **three** ways in which acid rains impacts the environment.

(a) _____

_____

_____

(b) _____

_____

_____

(c) _____

_____

_____

12. List and explain **three** actions we could take to reduce acid rain.

(a) _____

_____

_____

(b) _____

_____

_____

(c) _____

_____

_____

6 Weathering and Mass Movement:
The changing face of the Earth

1. Match the following terms with their correct definitions.

Weathering	This is a form of chemical weathering that occurs when carbon dioxide in the atmosphere mixes with rainwater to form a weak acid.
Erosion	This is a type of mechanical weathering that occurs in mountainous areas where there is a lot of precipitation and temperatures fall below freezing point.
Carbonation	This is the breaking down of rocks in an area where they are exposed to the weather. The broken-down material remains in this area.
Freeze-thaw action	This means the breaking down of rocks and the removal of their particles. When the material is broken down, it is transported elsewhere and deposited.

2. Name a type of mechanical weathering and explain, with the aid of a labelled diagram, how this type of weathering occurs.

Name: _____

Diagram

Explanation: _____

_____

_____

_____

3. Name a type of chemical weathering and explain, with the aid of a labelled diagram, how this type of weathering occurs.

Name: _____

> **Diagram**
>
>
>
>
>
>
>
>
>
>
>

Explanation: _____

_____

_____

_____

_____

4. What is a karst landscape? Give **two** examples of places where this type of landscape can be found.

_____

_____

_____

_____

5. Explain, with the aid of a diagram and using the D-E-P-E-D formula, the formation of **one** surface
feature you have studied that can be found in the Burren.

Name: _____

_____

Description: _____

Explanation: _____

_____

_____

_____

Processes: _____

_____

Example: _____

Diagram

6. Explain, with the aid of a diagram and using the D-E-P-E-D formula, the formation of **one** underground feature you have studied that can be found in the Burren.

Name: _____

_____

Description: _____

Explanation: _____

_____

_____

_____

Processes: _____

_____

Example: _____

Diagram

---

7. Who would be interested in visiting the Burren? List **four** examples.

(a) _____   (c) _____

(b) _____   (d) _____

8. Give **two** arguments in favour of tourism in the Burren.

(a) _____

_____

_____

(b) _____

_____

9. Give **two** arguments against tourism in the Burren.

(a) _____

_____

_____

(b) _____

_____

_____

10. Define the term 'regolith'.

_____

_____

11. List and describe **four** factors that affect mass movement.

(a) _____

_____

(b) _____

_____

(c) _____

_____

(d) _____

_____

12. Explain the following terms:

(a) Soil creep _____

_____

(b) Bog burst _____

_____

(c) Mudflow _____

_____

(d) Landslide _____

_____

(e) Avalanche _____

_____

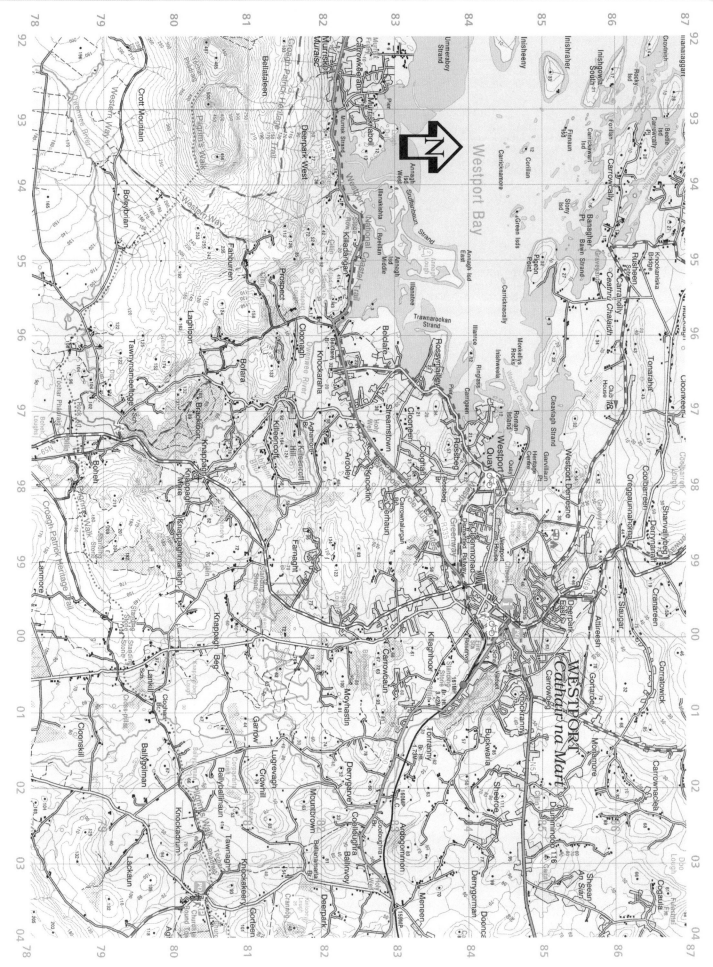

Examine the OS map, opposite, and aerial photograph, above, of Westport, and answer these questions.

1. Find the straight-line distance between the following points on the map:

(a) From the train station at M 006 840 to the post office at M 034 804

_____

(b) From the summit height at L 929 805 to the spot height (209 metres) at L 981 793

_____

(c) From the caravan park at L 986 853 to the youth hostel at M 006 841

_____

2. Find the curved-line distance of the following:

(a) The entire length of the railway line on the map

_____

(b) The length of the N 59 road

_____

(c) The length of the path named the Pilgrim's Walk

_____

3. Find the area of:

(a) The entire map extract

_____

(b) Westport Bay

_____

(c) The land east of the N 59

_____

(d) Land over 200 metres

_____

4. Give the name and grid reference of two slope types that you can identify on the OS map.

(a) _____

(b) _____

5. Use some of the words in the box below to write the correct name of each slope in the space provided under each diagram.

Concave slope   Convex slope   Even slope   Compound slope   Stepped slope

_____   _____   _____

6. Draw a cross-section from the spot height of 219 m at L 981 793 to the spot height of 124 m at L 967 793. Include features like roads and rivers on the cross-section.

7. Developers are planning on building a new shopping centre in the area of Westport. Using both the aerial photograph and the OS map, suggest a suitable location. Give **three** reasons to support your suggestion.

   (a) _____

   _____

   _____

   _____

   (b) _____

   _____

   _____

   _____

   (c) _____

   _____

   _____

   _____

8. What time of year was the photograph taken? Give reasons to justify your answer.

   _____

   _____

   _____

9. Is this a vertical or an oblique aerial photograph?

   _____

10. List **five** land uses that you can see on the aerial photograph. Give the location of each land use.

   (a) _____

   (b) _____

   (c) _____

   (d) _____

   (e) _____

11. Westport has a number of traffic management strategies in place. Identify these strategies in the aerial photograph and/or OS map and complete the following:

Strategy 1: _____

OS/Aerial: _____

Location: _____

Role: _____

_____

_____

Strategy 2: _____

OS/Aerial: _____

Location: _____

Role: _____

_____

_____

Strategy 3: _____

OS/Aerial: _____

Location: _____

Role: _____

_____

_____

12. €120 has been shared using the ratios in the table on the left. Match the ratios with the correct amounts of money in the table on the right by inserting the correct letter.

A	5:7
B	3:2
C	5:1
D	5:3
E	8:7

€100 & €20	
€75 & €45	
€72 & €48	
€64 & €56	
€50 & €70	

13. The table below shows the monthly temperature and rainfall figures for a town in India.

Month	Jan	Feb	Mar	Apr	May	Jun	Jul	Aug	Sep	Oct	Nov	Dec
Rainfall in mm	20	80	125	175	235	300	385	300	250	150	50	20
Temp in °C	24	27	32	36	34	33	32	30	30	29	28	26

(a) Name the wettest month.

_____

(b) Calculate the annual temperature range.

_____

14. The table below shows the average rainfall and temperature for an Irish town in 2015.

Month	Jan	Feb	Mar	Apr	May	Jun	Jul	Aug	Sep	Oct	Nov	Dec
Rainfall in mm	97.4	42.4	15.4	75.4	55.1	175.1	122.1	129.1	62.0	90.9	68.3	25.4
Temp in °C	5.8	6.6	7.9	6.7	10.5	13.0	13.9	15.4	11.8	8.0	5.5	2.9

(a) Find the mean temperature for the 12 months of the year.

_____

(b) Find the mean level of precipitation for the 12 months of the year.

_____

8 Secondary Economic Activities:
Industry in Ireland

1. Define the following terms:

    (a) Raw material:

    (b) Semi-finished product:

    (c) Finished product:

    (d) Manufacturing:

2. List and explain the factors that influence the location of a factory, using the sample answer on raw materials below as a guide.

    (a) Raw materials:

    Factories may choose to locate close to the source of the raw materials they use. If the raw materials are big and heavy, it will be easier and cheaper to transport them to a factory close to the source. If the raw materials are heavy, a factory may choose to locate near a port to make transport easier.

    (b) Markets:

    (c) Transport facilities:

    (d) Labour force:

(e) Services:

_____

_____

_____

_____

(f) Government/EU policy: _____

_____

_____

_____

(g) Personal preferences: _____

_____

_____

_____

3. Match the type of manufacturing industry with the correct definition.

Heavy industry	In this type of industry, the products being made are small and light. Electronic products and healthcare products are examples.
Light industry	These days, many manufacturing industries can set up in a variety of locations. They are not tied to one place.
MNCs	In this type of industry, the raw materials and the products being made are big and heavy. Iron and steel making are examples.
Footloose	These types of companies make their products in many different countries. Their headquarters are located in one country and they have branches in other countries throughout the world.

4. Fill in the information about a heavy industry you have studied.

Name of heavy industry	
Location	
Raw materials	
Process	
Output	
Transport	
Labour force	

5. Fill in the information about a light industry you have studied.

Name of light industry	
Location	
Output	
Transport	
Labour force	
Corporation tax	

6. Explain **two** reasons why a factory might choose to locate in an industrial estate.

(a) _____

_____

_____

(b) _____

_____

_____

1. Label the diagram below.

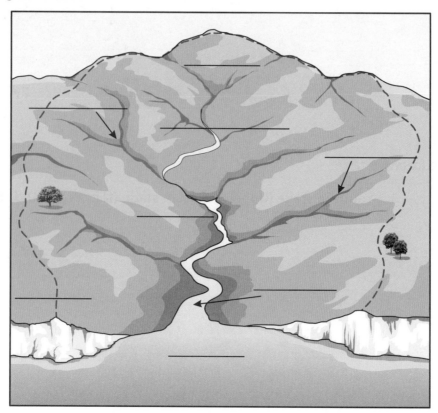

2. Define the following terms:

(a) Source: _____

_____

_____

(b) Course: _____

_____

_____

(c) Confluence: _____

_____

_____

(d) Tributary: _____

_____

_____

(e) Mouth: _____

_____

_____

(f) Drainage basin: _____

_____

_____

(g) Watershed: _____

_____

_____

(h) Estuary: _____

_____

_____

3. Complete the following table:

	Youthful stage (Upper)	Mature stage (Middle)	Old stage (Lower)
Gradient			
Speed			
Water quantity			
Erosion/Deposition			
Landforms			

4. Draw the following rivers on the map:

Shannon	Suir
Corrib	Nore
Moy	Barrow
Lee	Slaney
Liffey	

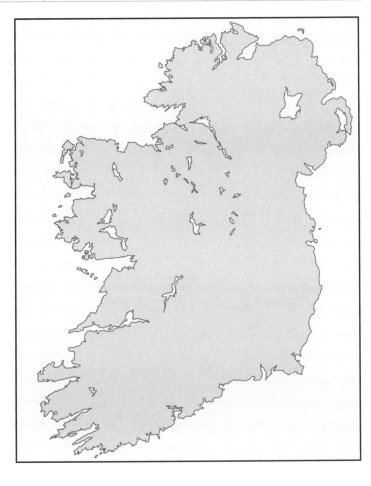

5. Define the following terms:

(a) Erosion: _____

_____

_____

(b) Transportation: _____

_____

_____

(c) Deposition: _____

_____

_____

6. Match the process of erosion with the correct definition.

Hydraulic action	Small stones carried by the river wear away the banks and the bed of the river.
Abrasion	Rocks such as limestone and soil are dissolved in the water.
Attrition	The force of the moving water wears away the banks and the bed of the river.
Solution	The small stones in the river are worn down and broken up as they hit off each other.

7. Label the diagram of river transportation processes below.

8. Explain **four** reasons why a river will deposit its load.

(a) _____

_____

_____

(b) _____

_____

_____

(c) _____

_____

_____

(d) _____

_____

_____

9. Using the D-E-P-E-D formula, explain how **one** landform of river erosion is formed.

Name: _____

Description: _____

Explanation: _____

_____

_____

_____

_____

Processes: _____

_____

Example: _____

Diagram

10. Identify this landform of river deposition.

_____

11. Using the D-E-P-E-D formula, explain how **one** feature of river deposition is formed.

Name: _____

Description: _____

Explanation: _____

_____

_____

_____

_____

_____

Processes: _____

_____

Example: _____

Diagram

12. Label the following diagram.

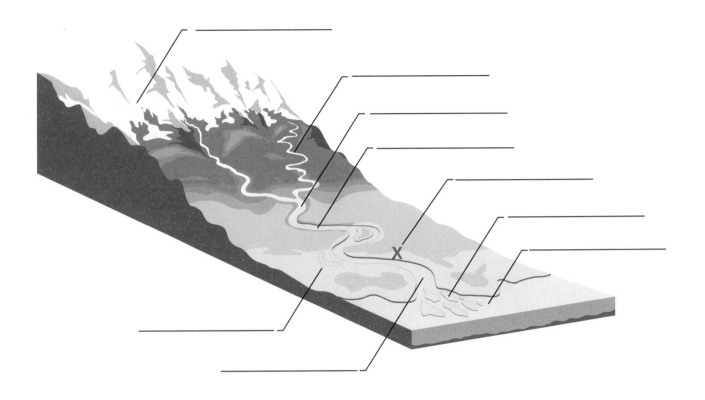

Mouth	Confluence	Levee
Source	Delta	Estuary
Tributary	Oxbow lake	Meander

13. Describe **one** way in which rivers can have a positive impact on humans.

14. Describe **one** way in which rivers can have a negative impact on humans.

10 The Sea:
How it shapes our coastline

1. Look at the following statements about how a wave comes ashore. Put the statements in the correct order, numbered 1–5.

The water returning out is known as the backwash.	
When waves reach shallow water they break and move towards the shore.	
When a wave breaks the water rushes up the shore.	
Waves are formed by the wind moving across the surface of the sea.	
The water coming in is known as the swash.	

2. Fill in the information about waves in the table below.

Type of wave	Destructive waves	Constructive waves
Diagram		
Description		
Causes erosion or deposition?		

3. Match the following processes of erosion with the correct definition.

Compression	Some rocks, such as limestone and chalk, are dissolved by water.
Hydraulic action	Loose material (rocks and sand) is thrown against the coastline by the waves. This action breaks more material off the coastline.
Attrition	When waves crash against a cliff, air gets trapped in the cracks and joints on the cliff face and becomes compressed. When the waves retreat, the pressure is suddenly released. This process of compression and release happens repeatedly until the rock eventually shatters.
Abrasion	The physical force of the waves breaks material off the coastline. During a storm, waves are stronger and their ability to erode increases.
Solution	The stones that are carried in the water are constantly hitting against each other. Over time they become worn down, smooth and rounded. This can eventually lead to the formation of sand.

4. Name **four** features of coastal erosion.

(a) _____

(b) _____

(c) _____

(d) _____

5. Using the D-E-P-E-D formula, explain how **one** landform of coastal erosion is formed.

Name: _____

Description: _____

Explanation: _____

_____

_____

_____

_____

_____

Processes: _____

_____

_____

Example: _____

The Sea: How it shapes our coastline

Diagram

6. Label the diagram below.

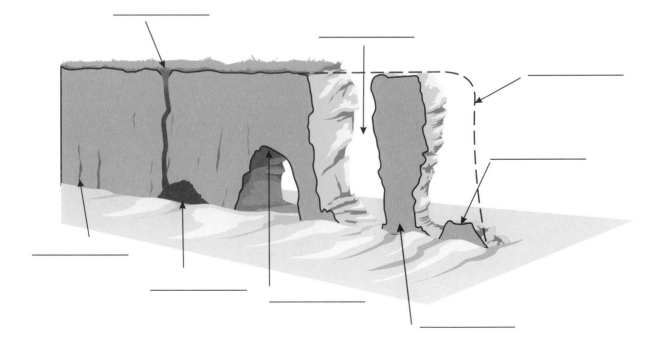

7. In the box below draw a labelled diagram to show how longshore drift occurs.

Diagram

8. Name **four** landforms of coastal deposition.

(a) _____

(b) _____

(c) _____

(d) _____

9. Using the D-E-P-E-D formula, explain how **one** landform of coastal deposition is formed.

Name: _____

Description: _____

Explanation: _____

_____

_____

_____

_____

_____

Processes: _____

_____

Example: _____

Diagram

10. Label the photograph below.

11. Name **two** ways in which people use coastal areas for their benefit. Explain each statement.

(a) Statement: _____

Explanation: _____

_____

Development: _____

_____

(b) Statement: _____

Explanation: _____

_____

Development: _____

_____

12. Describe **two** ways that people can have a negative impact on coastal areas.

(a) Statement: _____

Explanation: _____

_____

Development: _____

_____

(b) Statement: _____

_____

Explanation: _____

_____

Development: _____

_____

13. Fill out the information about coastal management in the table below.

Photograph	Name of coastal defence	How it works

11 Glaciation:
The work of ice

1. What is an ice age?

2. When did the last ice age end?

3. Explain why an ice age occurs.

4. Define the following processes of glacial erosion:

    (a) Plucking:

    (b) Abrasion:

5. Name **six** landforms of glacial erosion.

    (a)

    (b)

    (c)

    (d)

    (e)

    (f)

6. Match the landform of glacial erosion with the correct description.

Arête		Long narrow lake on the floor of a U-shaped valley
Ribbon lake		Basin-shaped hollow in a mountain that looks like an armchair
Cirque		Steep-sided peak between three or more cirques
Pyramidal peak		Narrow, steep-sided ridge that occurs between two cirques

7. Using the D-E-P-E-D formula, explain how **one** landform of glacial erosion is formed.

Name: _____

Description: _____

Explanation: _____

_____

_____

_____

_____

_____

Processes: _____

_____

Example: _____

Diagram

8. Label the diagram below.

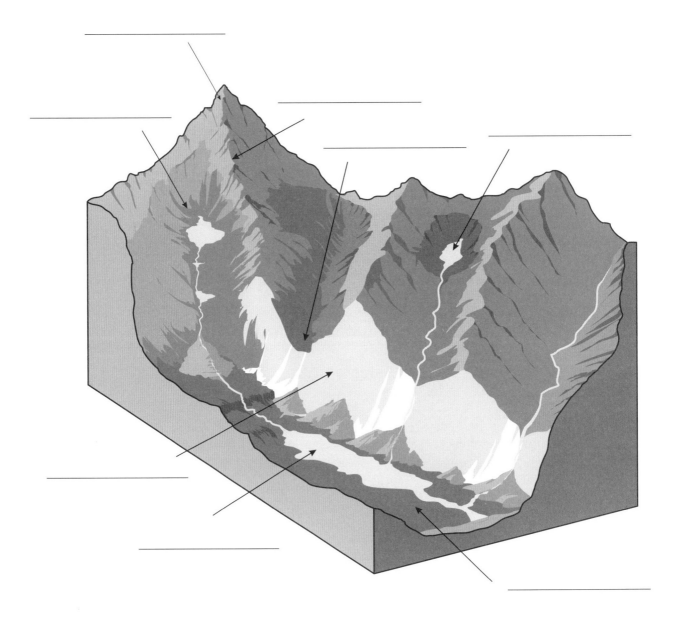

Corrie/Cirque	Hanging valley
Pyramidal Peak	Truncated spur
Arête	Ribbon lake
Corrie lake/Tarn	U-shaped valley

9. Name **three** landforms of glacial deposition.

(a) _____

(b) _____

(c) _____

10. Using the D-E-P-E-D formula, explain how **one** landform of glacial deposition is formed.

Name:

Description:

Explanation:

Processes:

Example:

Diagram

11. Name **two** landforms of glacial meltwater (fluvio-glacial) deposition.

(a) _____

(b) _____

12. Describe **two** ways in which glaciation has a positive impact on humans.

(a) _____

_____

_____

(b) _____

_____

_____

13. Describe **two** ways in which glaciation has a negative impact on humans.

(a) _____

_____

_____

(b) _____

_____

_____

12 Settlement and Urbanisation:
Where we live and why

1. List **four** physical factors that influence the site of a settlement.

   (a) _____   (c) _____

   (b) _____   (d) _____

2. List **four** factors that influence the situation of a settlement

   (a) _____   (c) _____

   (b) _____   (d) _____

3. List **four** categories of settlements throughout history.

   (a) _____   (c) _____

   (b) _____   (d) _____

4. List some antiquities or evidence of Celtic, Viking and Norman settlements that we might expect to see in the Irish landscape. Give at least **one** example from each of these periods.

_____

_____

_____

_____

5. List **seven** functions of urban settlements and give a named example of each.

   (a) Function: _____

        Example: _____

   (b) Function: _____

        Example: _____

   (c) Function: _____

        Example: _____

   (d) Function: _____

        Example: _____

   (e) Function: _____

        Example: _____

   (f) Function: _____

        Example: _____

   (g) Function: _____

        Example: _____

6. (a) Name a city whose function has changed over time.

_____

(b) Explain **three** functions that this city had in the past or has currently.

(i) _____

_____

(ii) _____

_____

(iii) _____

_____

7. (a) 'This area has a long history of settlement.' Discuss this statement using **three** examples from the OS map opposite.

(i) _____

_____

_____

(ii) _____

_____

_____

(iii) _____

_____

_____

(b) List and explain **two** reasons why Dungarvan developed at this location.

(i) _____

_____

_____

(ii) _____

_____

_____

(c) Using the OS map, describe how the functions of Dungarvan have changed over time.

_____

_____

_____

_____

_____

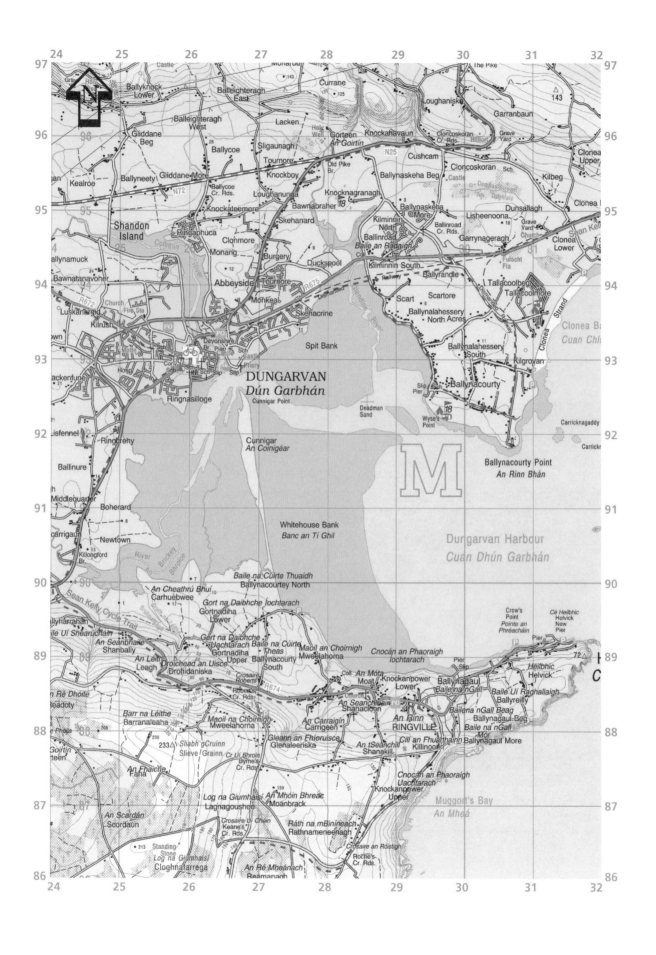

8. Choose a town or city near you and complete the table below.

Name of town/city	
Past functions of the area	
Present functions of the area	

9. Fill in the table below with information about settlement patterns.

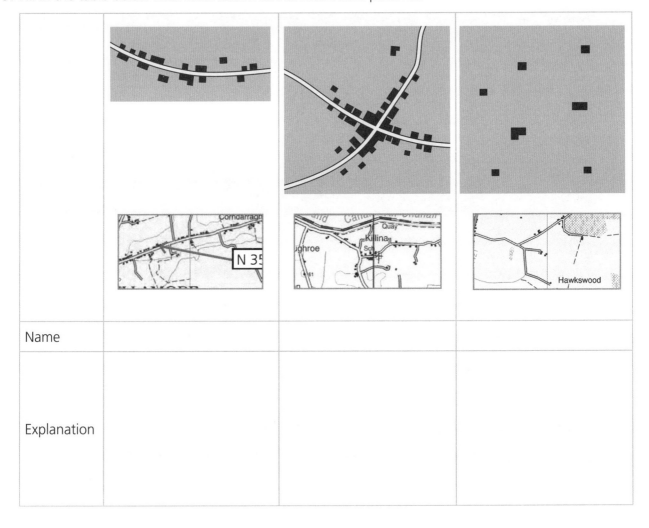

Name			
Explanation			

10. Define the term 'urbanisation'.

_____

_____

_____

11. Define the following terms:

(a) Commuters:

_____

_____

_____

(b) Rush hour:

_____

_____

_____

(c) Traffic congestion:

_____

_____

_____

(d) Public transport:

_____

_____

_____

12. Define the following terms in relation to Dublin's urban problems:

(a) Zones of decline:

_____

_____

_____

(b) Urban sprawl:

_____

_____

_____

(c) Unemployment:

_____

_____

_____

(d) Crime:

_____

_____

_____

_____

13. List and explain **two** ways in which Dublin has tried to solve traffic congestion.

(a) _____

_____

_____

(b) _____

_____

_____

14. List and explain the **five** functional zones that can be seen in cities.

(a) Name: _____

Explain: _____

_____

_____

(b) Name: _____

Explain: _____

_____

_____

(c) Name: _____

Explain: _____

_____

_____

(d) Name: _____

Explain: _____

_____

_____

(e) Name: _____

Explain: _____

_____

_____

15. Label the diagram below.

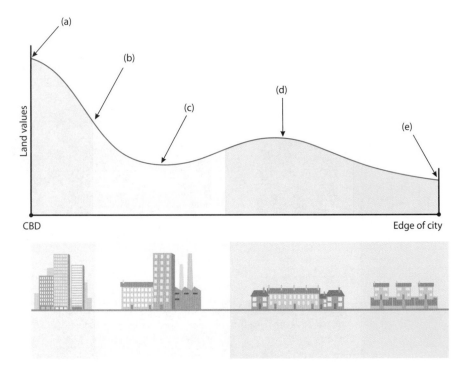

(a) _____

_____

(b) _____

_____

(c) _____

_____

(d) _____

_____

(e) _____

_____

16. Identify the type of residential housing in each photograph.

17.

(a) What type of photograph is this?

(b) Identify what time of year this photograph was taken and give reasons for your answer.

_____

_____

_____

_____

(c) Can you locate the following urban land uses on the photograph?

    (i)   Recreational   _____

    (ii)   Residential   _____

    (iii) Industrial   _____

    (iv) Commercial   _____

    (v)   Tourism   _____

    (vi) Health   _____

    (vii) Ecclesiastical   _____

(d) Locate and explain **two** ways in which traffic has been managed in the photograph.

    (i) _____

    _____

    (ii) _____

    _____

(e) It is proposed that a new shopping centre be built in the town. Where would you locate it? Give **two** reasons to justify your answer.

    (i) _____

    _____

    _____

    (ii) _____

    _____

    _____

Settlement and Urbanisation: Where we live and why

1. Name **three** gases present in the atmosphere.

(a) _____

(b) _____

(c) _____

2. Define the following terms:

(a) Stratosphere: _____

(b) Troposphere: _____

(c) Solar radiation: _____

3. Name the line that divides the northern hemisphere and the southern hemisphere.

_____

4. Name the lines that measure the distance from the equator.

_____

5. True or false?

(a) Air that heats and rises creates an area of high pressure.

_____

(b) Winds blow from areas of high pressure to areas of low pressure.

_____

(c) The air that moves from the equator is cold air.

_____

6. Label the diagram on the right.

(a) _____

(b) _____

(c) _____

(d) _____

(e) _____

(f) _____

7. Explain the term 'Coriolis effect'.

_____

_____

_____

8. Name each current in the diagram on the right.

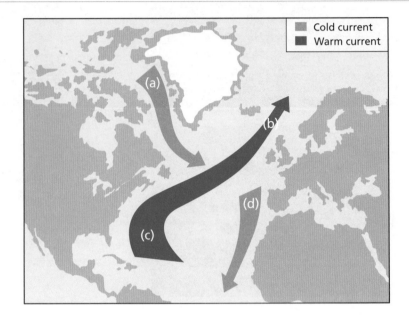

Cold current
Warm current

(a) _____

(b) _____

(c) _____

(d) _____

9. Explain the term 'air masses' and give three examples.

_____

_____

_____

_____

10. Explain the following terms:

(a) Isobars: _____

_____

_____

_____

(b) Fronts: _____

_____

_____

_____

(c) Millibars: _____

_____

_____

11. Label each cloud type.

(a) _____

(b) _____

(c) _____

12. Name a type of rainfall other than relief rainfall, and explain how it occurs with the aid of a diagram.

_____

_____

_____

_____

Diagram

13. Label the diagram using the following terms: warm air, condenses, relief rain, rain shadow.

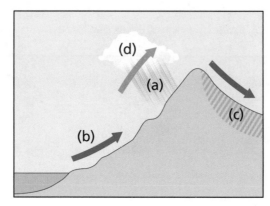

(a) _____

(b) _____

(c) _____

(d) _____

14. Name the **seven** elements of weather that are measured constantly.

(a) _____

(b) _____

(c) _____

(d) _____

(e) _____

(f) _____

(g) _____

15. What is the name of the person who prepares the weather forecast?

_____

16. Why is the weather forecast important to us?

_____

_____

_____

17. What is the name of the meteorological service in Ireland?

_____

18. What are synoptic maps?

_____

_____

_____

Weather: How it impacts on our lives

19. Fill in the table. Begin by naming the instruments and what they measure.

Instrument						
What it measures						
Unit of measurement						
How it is shown on a synoptic map						

Climates:
Classifying climate types and Ireland's climate

1. Distinguish between weather and climate.

_____

_____

_____

2. Name and explain **three** factors that influence climate.

(a) _____

_____

_____

(b) _____

_____

_____

(c) _____

_____

_____

3. Is it colder at (a) or (b)? Explain why.

_____

_____

_____

4. Explain why it is colder in Zurich than it is in Dublin in the winter.

_____

_____

_____

_____

_____

5. Explain the term 'prevailing winds' and name Ireland's prevailing winds.

_____

_____

6. Explain the following terms:

   (a) Aspect: _____

                 _____

   (b) Altitude: _____

                 _____

7. Is it colder at (a) or (b)? Explain why.

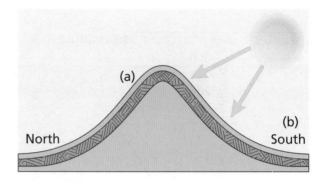

North   South

8. Equatorial climate

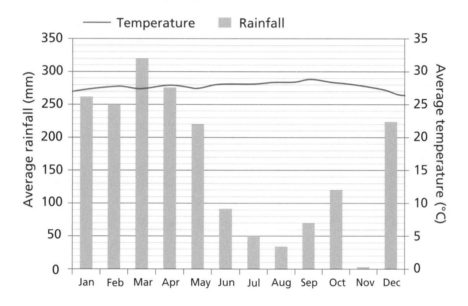

(a) What was the average rainfall in March?

_____

(b) What was the average rainfall in September?

_____

(c) What was the mean average rainfall for the first three months of the year?

_____

(d) What was the total rainfall for June, July and August?

_____

(e) Explain why there was little variation in the temperature throughout the year.

_____

_____

_____

Climates: Classifying climate types and Ireland's climate

9. Savannah climate

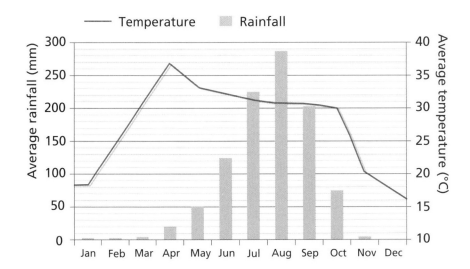

(a) Which month has the highest temperature?

_____

(b) What was the average temperature in September?

_____

(c) What was the mean monthly rainfall for June, July and August?

_____

10. Examine the diagram below. Name **four** countries that have hot desert regions.

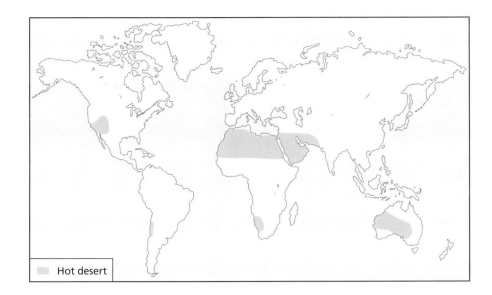

(a) _____

(b) _____

(c) _____

(d) _____

11. Draw a diagram illustrating the greenhouse effect, and explain it in the space below.

Diagram

Explanation: _____

_____

_____

_____

_____

_____

_____

1. Draw a sketch map of the aerial photograph of Tullamore above. Include the following:

   (a) Main street

   (b) Residential land use

   (c) Commercial land use

   (d) Two traffic management strategies

   (e) The Grand Canal

   (f) Recreational land use.

N

Kilnacking
Cartron
Whiteforge Cross Rds
Mound
Durrow Demesne
Tara
Keeloge
Durrow Abbey
Motte
Durrow Church & High Cross
Balleek Beg
Castle
Frevanagh
Ballybroder
Ballycallaghan
Derrygolan
Ashfield
Coniker
Balleek
Loughaun
Durrow Cross Rds
Ballynamona
Derrygolan Br
Coolnahely
62MP
Coolnahely Br
Mound
Tihilly Church & High Cross
Kildangan
Lug
Acantha
Cartron East
Silver River
Abhainn Airgid
Gormagh
Ballynasrah or Tinnycross
Aharney
Culleen
Coleraine
Gormagh Br
Moleen
Rosnagowloge or Tirinchinan
Ballyooshey
61MP
Ballyduff Br
Castle
Muiniagh
Ardan
Derrynagall or Ballydaly
Ballykilmurry
Castle
Ballyduff
Corndarragh
Hut site
60MP
TULLAMORE
Tulach Mhór
Ballynamire House
Ballydrohid Br
Srah
Puttaghan
Digby
25th Lock
54
Killiskea Cross Rds
Standing Stone
59MP
Cartron West
Ballydrohid
26th Lock
Bogtown
Kilbride
Church
Grand Canal Way
Castle
Fortified House
29th Lock
Slíne Canálach Móire
28th Lock
Ballycowan Br
Ballycowan
Tullamore River
Killiskea
58MP
Br.Ht. 4.14m
Kilgortin
Kilcruttin
Ballynagh
Tullamore River
R420
Annamoe Br
Holy Well
Cloncollog
Barony
Lynally Glebe
Motte
Charleville Demesne
Spollanstown
Church
Charleville Castle
Ballard
Gayfield
57MP
56MP
Cloghabrack
Muclagh Br
N52
Clonminch
Fertaun
Holy Well
Mucklagh
An Muclach
Claragh
Screggan
An Screagán
Glash Br
Cloncon
Earthworks
Brookfield
Haras Hill
Heath
Cloghanbane
Blackagh
Clonagh East
Killeenmore
Earthwork
Derryclure
Shanvally
Ross
Clonagh West
Derrybeg
Graigue
Hawkswood

2. Look at the OS map (page 75) and the aerial photograph (page 74) of Tullamore.
Give **three** examples of how they show information about an area in different ways.

(a) _____

_____

_____

_____

(b) _____

_____

_____

_____

(c) _____

_____

_____

_____

3. Use the OS map and the aerial photograph to identify what direction the camera was facing/
pointing when the photograph was taken.

_____

4. Insert the correct letter A to D in the boxes below, to identify each of the images.

 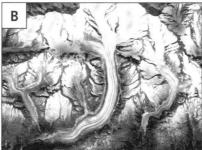 

Description	Letter
A flowing glacier in Switzerland	
Hydroelectric power station	
Niagara Falls, Canada	
Trim Castle, Co. Meath	

5. Examine the satellite images and answer each of the following questions.

(a) Insert the correct letter A to D in the boxes below, to identify each of the images.

Description	Letter
Airport runway	
Pyramids in Egypt	
Grand Canyon	
Flooding	

(b) State **one** use of satellite images.

_____

6. Insert the correct letter A to D in the boxes below, to identify each of the images.

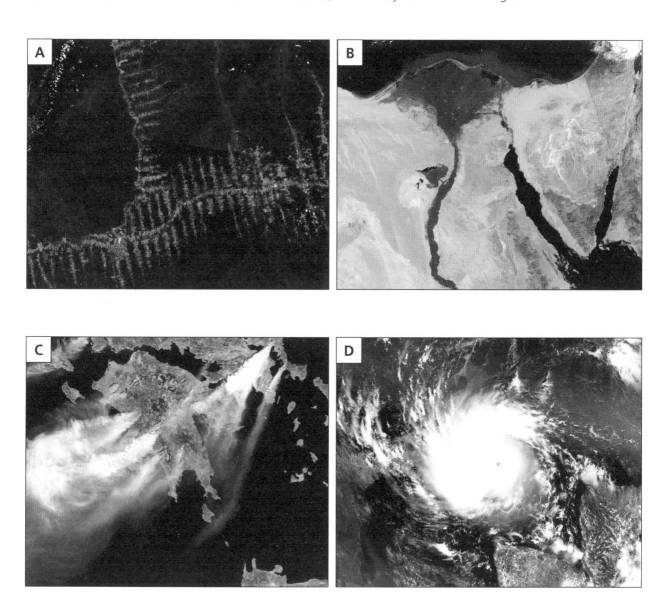

Description	Letter
Hurricane	
Deforestation	
Bush Fires	
Delta	

7. Insert the correct letter A to E in the boxes below, to identify each of the images.

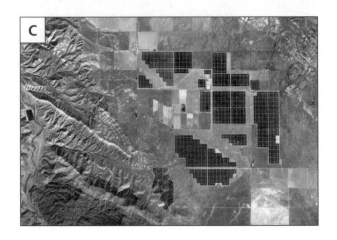

Description	Letter
Solar power plant in the desert	
Before and after Japan tsunami 2011	
Copacabana Beach, Rio de Janeiro	
Atlantic storm	

8. Draw a sketch map of the Carlow OS map and include the following:

(a) Urban area of Carlow   (c) River Barrow   (e) County boundary

(b) Area over 200 m   (d) Motorway   (f) Railway line

9. Four-figure grid references

(a) Name the two types of road that meet at S 70 69.

_____

_____

(b) What building is located at S 71 74? _____

(c) Name the town land located at S 72 71. _____

(d) Give the four-figure grid reference for:

(i) an area of coniferous plantation. _____

(ii) the townland of Johnduffswood. _____

10. Six-figure grid references

   (a) What antiquity is located at S 719 709? _____

   (b) What is the name of the bridge at S 700 705? _____

   (c) What transport feature is located at S 726 772? _____

   (d) Give the six-figure grid reference for the following:

      (i)   Where the River Barrow meets the Fushoge River _____

      (ii) The summit height/triangulation pillar of 336 m _____

      (iii) The reservoir _____

11. Area

   (a) Calculate the area for the entire map extract. _____

   (b) Calculate the area for the land over 200 m. _____

   (c) What is the area of land west of the River Barrow
        on the extract? _____

12. Distance

   (a) What is the straight-line distance between the church at
        Nurney S 73 67 and the church at Cloonaloo S 67 77? _____

   (b) What is the length of the county boundary shown on the map? _____

   (c) What is the length of the railway line on the map? _____

13. Direction

   (a) What direction would you be travelling if you left Carlow Town
        on the R448 to get onto the motorway? _____

   (b) What direction would you be travelling if you left Carlow Town
        on the R430 going towards Clonmore? _____

   (c) If you were on top of the summit at S 669 741 and looked
        towards Carlow Town, in which direction would you be looking? _____

14. Height

List **four** ways height is shown on OS maps. Use examples and locations from the Carlow Ordnance
Survey map.

_____

_____

_____

_____

15. Slope

(a) What type of slope is located at S 66 76? _____

(b) What type of slope is located at S 67 74? _____

16. Draw a cross-section from the spot height of 318 m at S 674 723 to the church at S 688 729.

Aerial Photograph

17. What type of photograph is this? _____

18. Draw a sketch map of the aerial photograph of Carlow and include the following:

(a) The river

(b) A bridge

(c) A residential area

(d) An industrial area

(e) A recreational area

(f) An agricultural area

19. At what time of year do you think the photograph was taken? Give reasons for your answer.

_____

_____

_____

_____

20. Distinguish **four** land uses/functions on the photograph and give their location.

(a) _____

_____

(b) _____

_____

(c) _____

_____

(d) _____

_____

21. Look at the OS map and the aerial photograph. Identify and describe **three** differences that you can see from studying the two.

(a) _____

_____

_____

(b) _____

_____

_____

(c) _____

_____

_____

22. What direction was the camera facing when the photograph was taken?

_____

16 Soil:
A vital natural resource

1. Label each section in the pie chart with the ingredients of soil and the percentage (%) of each ingredient.

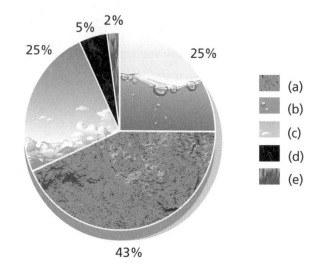

(a) _____

(b) _____

(c) _____

(d) _____

(e) _____

2. Circle the correct term in the statements below.

   (a) The main ingredient in soil is **living organisms / mineral matter**.

   (b) Air containing **nitrogen / carbon dioxide** is vital for living organisms in the soil to survive.

   (c) Water makes up about **25 per cent / 20 per cent** of soil.

   (d) Humus is a **dark / light** jelly-like substance.

   (e) Humus provides the soil with **nutrients / dissolved minerals**.

3. Match the following terms with the correct descriptions.

Living organisms	It is made up of rock particles that have been weathered and eroded. It includes stones, sand, silt and clay, and provides the minerals that help plants to grow.
Humus	It contains oxygen and nitrogen, which are vital for plants to grow, and for living organisms to survive in the soil.
Mineral matter	It makes up about 25 per cent of soil and helps to bind the soil together. Minerals dissolved in water are absorbed through the roots of plants and help them grow.
Water	It is a dark, jelly-like substance that forms when the living organisms in the soil break down the remains of decayed plants and animals.
Air	These are earthworms and various bacteria, fungi, insects and burrowing animals. These break down the organic matter to form humus, and mix up the soil to make it easier for water and air to pass through.

4. Explain the terms below and then draw and label a soil profile in the space provided.

(a) Top soil

(b) Subsoil

(c) Bedrock

Soil Profile

5. Explain the term 'leaching' and the problems it can cause.

_____

_____

_____

_____

6. List the **six** factors that influence soil formation.

(a) _____

(b) _____

(c) _____

(d) _____

(e) _____

(f) _____

7. Explain **three** of the factors that influence soil formation.

(a) _____

_____

(b) _____

_____

(c) _____

_____

8. Look at the map of Ireland. Where are the following soil types predominately found?

(a) Gley soils

_____

(b) Brown earth soils

_____

(c) Peaty soils

_____

(d) Podzol soils

_____

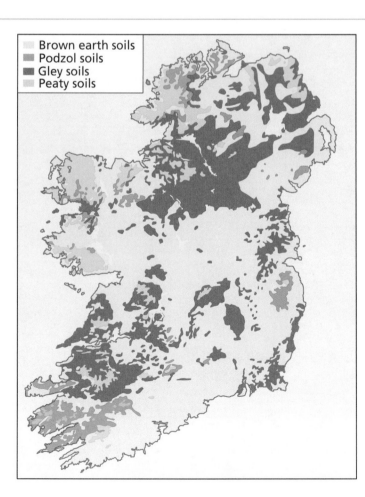

Brown earth soils
Podzol soils
Gley soils
Peaty soils

Soil: A vital natural resource

89

9. Fill in the table below.

	Soil type	Location	How it was formed	Is there much humus?	Is it fertile?	Is it well drained?	Does leaching occur?	Is it good for agriculture?
Brown earth soils								
Podzol soils								
Gley soils								
Peaty soils								

10. The relationship between soil and the vegetation that grows in it is very important.

(a) Describe how soil influences vegetation.

_____

_____

_____

_____

(b) Describe how vegetation influences soil.

_____

_____

_____

_____

11. List and explain **two** ways in which humans have a negative impact on soil.

(a) _____

_____

_____

(b) _____

_____

_____

12. List **three** differences between raised bogs and blanket bogs.

(a) _____

_____

(b) _____

_____

(c) _____

_____

13. What is the name of the government company set up to exploit peat in Ireland?

_____

Soil: A vital natural resource

17 Tertiary Economic Activities:
Transport and tourism

1. Name **four** regions in Ireland that offer various attractions to tourists and give examples of attractions for each region.

   (a) _____

   _____

   (b) _____

   _____

   (c) _____

   _____

   (d) _____

   _____

2. List and explain **three** reasons for the growth of tourism in recent years, both in Ireland and around the world.

   (a) _____

   _____

   (b) _____

   _____

   (c) _____

   _____

3. Choose a tourist attraction in Ireland with which you are familiar. Describe **three** reasons why this location attracts tourists.

Name	
Reason 1	
Reason 2	
Reason 3	

4. Mark **five** different tourist
attractions on the map on the
right, one in each province and one
in Dublin.

5. Define the term 'ecotourism'.

_____

_____

_____

6. List and explain **three** impacts tourism has on the landscape.

(a) _____

_____

(b) _____

_____

(c) _____

_____

7. Explain **two** social or economic improvements that can occur due to tourism.

(a) _____

_____

(b) _____

_____

8. List **four** projects carried out by the government to improve transport in Ireland.

(a) _____

(b) _____

(c) _____

(d) _____

9. Mark the following motorways in blue on the map below.

(a) M1

(b) M4/M6

(c) M7

(d) M8

(e) M9

(f) M11

(g) M17/18

(h) M50

10. Explain **two** ways in which the physical landscape impacts on the construction of transport links.

(a) _____

_____

(b) _____

_____

11. How is tourism impacted by transport in a region?

_____

_____

_____

18 Population:
How population changes over time

1. Population growth

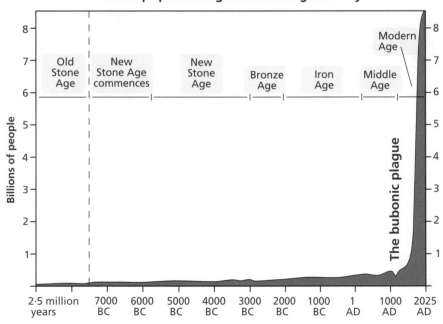

World population growth through history

(a) Give **two** reasons why the world's population has fluctuated throughout history.

_____

_____

(b) Explain the rapid population growth that has occurred since 1750.

_____

_____

_____

2. Explain the following terms:

(a) Birth rate

_____

_____

_____

(b) Death rate

_____

_____

_____

(c) Migration

_____

_____

_____

(d) Natural increase

_____

_____

_____

(e) Natural decrease

_____

_____

_____

3. Name the factors that influence the rate of population change and explain each one.

(a) Name:

_____

Explanation:

_____

_____

_____

(b) Name:

_____

Explanation:

_____

_____

_____

(c) Name:

_____

Explanation:

_____

_____

_____

(d) Name:

_____

Explanation:

_____

_____

_____

(e) Name:

_____

Explanation:

_____

_____

_____

(f) Name:

_____

Explanation:

_____

_____

_____

4. The population cycle

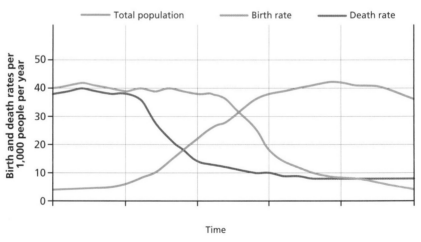

(a) Name **each** of the five stages of the population cycle.

(i) _____

(ii) _____

(iii) _____

(iv) _____

(v) _____

(b) Why are the birth and death rates high in Stage 1?

_____

_____

_____

(c) What causes the death rate to drop in Stage 2?

_____

_____

_____

(d) Why is the population increasing rapidly in Stage 3?

_____

_____

(e) What causes population growth to slow down in Stage 4?

_____

_____

_____

(f) Why does the population go into decline in Stage 5?

_____

_____

_____

5. What is the pessimistic view on population growth in the future?

_____

_____

_____

6. What is the optimistic view on population growth in the future?

_____

_____

_____

7. Population pyramids: Brazil and Germany

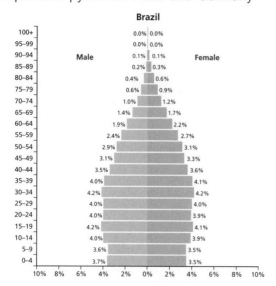

(a) What percentage of people are in the 0-9 age group in Brazil?

_____

(b) What percentage of people are in the 0-9 age group in Germany?

_____

(c) Can you explain the difference between the two figures?

_____

_____

_____

(d) Is life expectancy higher in Brazil or Germany? Refer to the population pyramids to support your answer.

_____

(f) Explain why there is a difference in life expectancy between the two countries.

_____

_____

_____

8. Give **three** reasons why population pyramids might be useful to governments and other agencies.

(a) _____

_____

_____

(b) _____

_____

Population: How population changes over time

(c) _____

_____

_____

9. Draw a population pyramid using the following estimated figures from the Central Statistics Office website for 2017.

Population estimates by age group and sex

Age Group		2017	Notes and workings
Both sexes			
0–14 years		21%	
15–24 years		12%	
25–44 years		29%	
45–64 years		24%	
65 years and over		14%	
Male			
0–14 years		11%	
15–24 years		6%	
25–44 years		14%	
45–64 years		12%	
65 years and over		6%	
All ages		49%	
Female			
0–14 years		10%	
15–24 years		6%	
25–44 years		15%	
45–64 years		12%	
65 years and over		8%	
All ages		51%	

10. Read the information on Ireland before and after the Great Famine on pages 333–334 of the textbook and answer the following questions:

(a) Explain **two** reasons why the population of Ireland was high in 1841.

_____

_____

_____

_____

(b) What caused the Great Famine of 1845–1852?

_____

_____

_____

_____

(c) Explain **two** immediate results of the famine.

_____

_____

_____

_____

(d) Explain **two** long-term effects of the famine.

_____

_____

_____

_____

Population: How population changes over time

1. Explain the following terms using examples you have studied:

(a) Internal migration

_____

_____

_____

(b) International migration

_____

_____

_____

(c) Individual migration

_____

_____

_____

(d) Push factors

_____

_____

_____

(e) Pull factors

_____

_____

_____

(f) Barriers to migration

_____

_____

_____

2. Describe **three** impacts of migration on the place left behind.

(a) _____

_____

_____

(b) _____

_____

_____

(c) _____

_____

_____

3. Describe **three** impacts of migration on the place people move to.

(a) _____

_____

_____

(b) _____

_____

_____

(c) _____

_____

_____

4. Name an organised migration you have studied and describe **three** of its effects.

Name	
Effect 1	
Effect 2	
Effect 3	

Migration: People on the move

103

20 Economic Inequality:
A world divided

1. Define the following terms and give examples:

   (a) Developed economies

   _____

   _____

   _____

   (b) Economies in transition

   _____

   _____

   _____

   (c) Developing economies

   _____

   _____

   _____

2. Look at the map below. Draw a line marking the North–South divide. Then colour developed areas in blue, areas in transition in orange and developing areas in red.

3. Explain the term 'Gross National Income' (GNI).

   _____

   _____

   _____

4. Explain the term 'Human Development Index' (HDI).

_____

_____

_____

5. Give **three** reasons for the economic divide that exists between the North and the South.

(a) Reason:

_____

Explanation:

_____

_____

_____

(b) Reason:

_____

Explanation:

_____

_____

_____

(c) Reason:

_____

Explanation:

_____

_____

_____

6. Name a commodity that is traded worldwide and a country that produces this commodity.

_____

_____

7. Explain the term 'fair trade'.

_____

_____

_____

8. Explain each of the following terms using examples:

(a) Bilateral aid

_____

_____

_____

(b) Multilateral aid

_____

_____

_____

(c) Non-government aid

_____

_____

_____

(d) Emergency/humanitarian aid

_____

_____

_____

(e) Development aid

_____

_____

_____

(f) Tied aid

_____

_____

_____

9. Name **three** Irish non-government organisations (NGOs).

_____

_____

_____

10. Read the case study on Ireland's overseas aid on pages 363–364 of the textbook and answer the following questions:

(a) Name the Irish programme for overseas aid.

_____

(b) Name a country to which the Irish government gives assistance. What is the population of that country?

_____

_____

(c) Briefly explain the work-for-food programme.

_____

_____

_____

(d) How much of the budget is spent on combatting HIV/AIDS?

_____

(e) Why is 6 per cent of the budget spent on governance issues?

_____

_____

_____

Economic Inequality: A world divided

21 Globalisation:
Living in an interconnected world

1. What does the term 'globalisation' mean?

_____

_____

_____

2. List **four** factors that influence globalisation.

(a) _____

(b) _____

(c) _____

(d) _____

3. Explain **two** of the factors that influence globalisation.

(a) _____

_____

_____

(b) _____

_____

_____

4. List and explain **two** negative impacts of globalisation.

(a) _____

_____

_____

_____

(b) _____

_____

_____

_____

5. How has globalisation influenced population change?

_____

_____

_____

_____

_____

_____

_____

6. Describe why globalisation will develop at an uneven rate.

_____

_____

_____

_____

_____

_____

_____

Globalisation: Living in an interconnected world